nd we give thanks to God, the Father of our Lord Jesus Christ. 4 For we have hea
n Christ Jesus and your love for all of God's people, 5 which come from your co
t God has reserved for you in heaven. You have had this expectation ever since
the truth of the Good News. 6 This same Good News that came to you is going out
it is bearing fruit everywhere by changing lives, just as it changed your lives
rst heard and understood the truth about God's wonderful grace. 7 You learned
rom Epaphras, our beloved co-worker. He is Christ's faithful servant, and he i
r behalf. 8 He has told us about the love for others that the Holy Spirit has gi
e not stopped praying for you since we first heard about you. We ask God to giv
edge of his will and to give you spiritual wisdom and understanding. 10 Then t
ill always honor and please the Lord, and your lives will produce every kind o
e while, you will grow as you learn to know God better and better. 11 We also pr
e strengthened with all his glorious power so you will have all the endurance
ed. May you h   e has enabled
 inheritance   *CHASING SACRED BIBLE STUDY*   3 For he has re
ngdom of dar   ar Son, 14 who
m and forgave our sins. 15 Christ is the visible image of the invisible God. He
ing was created and is supreme over all creation, 16 for through him God create
heavenly realms and on earth. He made the things we can see and the things w
s thrones, kingdoms, rulers, and authorities   world. Everything
h him and for him. 17 He existe   he holds all creati
t is also the head of the church,   beginning, suprem
rom the dead. So he is first in ev   his fullness was p
ist, 20 and through him God reco   everything to himself. He made peace w
ven and on earth by means of Christ's blood on the cross. 21 This includes you
ay from God. You were his enemies, separated from him by your evil thoughts a
 now he has reconciled you to himself through the death of Christ in his physi
lt, he has brought you into his own presence, and you are holy and blameless a
 him without a single fault. 23 But you must continue to believe this truth an
Don't drift away from the assurance you received when you heard the Good News
has been preached all over the world, and I, Paul, have been appointed as God's
im it. 24 I am glad when I suffer for you in my body, for I am participating in t
ist that continue for his body, the church. 25 God has given me the responsibil
urch by proclaiming his entire message to you. 26 This message was kept secre
nerations past, but now it has been revealed to God's people. 27 For God wanted
he riches and glory of Christ are for you Gentiles, too. And this is the secret:

we give thanks to God, the Father of our Lord Jesus Christ. 4 For we have hear
Christ Jesus and your love for all of God's people, 5 which come from your con
God has reserved for you in heaven. You have had this expectation ever since
the truth of the Good News. 6 This same Good News that came to you is going out
t is bearing fruit everywhere by changing lives, just as it changed your lives
st heard and understood the truth about God's wonderful grace. 7 You learned a
m Epaphras, our beloved co-worker. He is Christ's faithful servant, and he is
behalf. 8 He has told us about the love for others that the Holy Spirit has giv
not stopped praying for you since we first heard about you. We ask God to give
ge of his will and to give you spiritual wisdom and understanding. 10 Then the
l always honor and please the Lord, and your lives will produce every kind of
while, you will grow as you learn to know God better and better. 11 We also pra
strengthened with all his glorious power so you will have all the endurance a
d. May you be filled with joy, 12 always thanking the Father. He has enabled yo
nheritance that belongs to his people, who live in the light. 13 For he has resc
rdom of darkness and transferred us into the Kingdom of his dear Son, 14 who p
and forgave our sins. 15 Christ is the visible image of the invisible God. He e
g was created and is supreme over all creation, 16 for through him God created
eavenly realms and on earth. He made the things we can see and the things we
thrones, kingdoms, rulers, and authorities in the unseen world. Everything wa
him and for him. 17 He existed before anything else, and he holds all creatio
s also the head of the church, which is his body. He is the beginning, supreme
m the dead. So he is first in everything. 19 For God in all his fullness was ple
st, 20 and through him God reconciled everything to himself. He made peace wit
en and on earth by means of Christ's blood on the cross. 21 This includes you wh
from God. You were his enemies, separated from him by your evil thoughts and
ow he has reconciled you to himself through the death of Christ in his physica
, he has brought you into his own presence, and you are holy and blameless as
im without a single fault. 23 But you must continue to believe this truth and
on't drift away from the assurance you received when you heard the Good News.
s been preached all over the world, and I, Paul, have been appointed as God's s
m it. 24 I am glad when I suffer for you in my body, for I am participating in the
st that continue for his body, the church. 25 God has given me the responsibilit
rch by proclaiming his entire message to you. 26 This message was kept secret
erations past, but now it has been revealed to God's people. 27 For God wanted

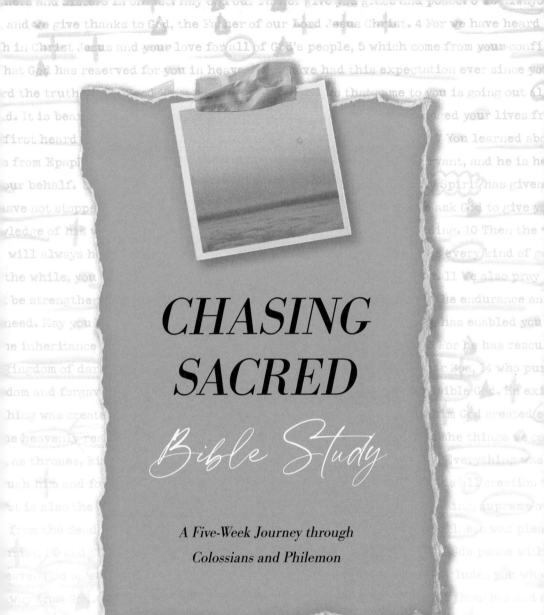

CHASING SACRED

Bible Study

A Five-Week Journey through
Colossians and Philemon

MIKELLA VAN DYKE

TYNDALE
MOMENTUM®

A Tyndale nonfiction imprint

Visit Tyndale online at tyndale.com.

Visit the author online at chasingsacred.com.

Tyndale, Tyndale's quill logo, *Tyndale Momentum*, and the Tyndale Momentum logo are registered trademarks of Tyndale House Ministries. Tyndale Momentum is a nonfiction imprint of Tyndale House Publishers, Carol Stream, Illinois.

Chasing Sacred Bible Study: A Five-Week Journey through Colossians and Philemon

Cover and interior photograph of sunset clouds by Charles Postiaux on Unsplash.com.

Cover design by Julie Chen

Published in association with the literary agency of Books & Such Literary Management, 52 Mission Circle, Suite 122, PMB 170, Santa Rosa, CA 95409.

For information about special discounts for bulk purchases, please contact Tyndale House Publishers at csresponse@tyndale.com, or call 1-855-277-9400.

ISBN 978-1-4964-8075-0

Printed in China

30	29	28	27	26	25	24
7	6	5	4	3	2	1

To my children:

Paxton, Barkley, Hudson, Copley, and Tatum.
You have expanded my heart and kept me laughing.

. we give thanks to God, the Father of our Lord Jesus Christ. 4 For we have heard

Christ Jesus and your love for all of God's people, 5 which come from your confi

God has reserved for you in heaven. You have had this expectation ever since yo

he truth of the Good News. 6 This same Good News that came to you is going out al

t is bearing fruit everywhere by changing lives, just as it changed your lives fr

t heard and understood the truth about God's wonderful grace. 7 You learned ab

om Epaphras, our beloved co-worker. He is Christ's faithful servant, and he is h

behalf. 8 He has told us about the love for others that the Holy Spirit has given

not stopped praying for you since we first heard about you. We ask God to give y

ge of his will and to give you spiritual wisdom and understanding. 10 Then the

l always honor and please the Lord, and your lives will produce every kind of g

while, you will grow as you learn to know God better and better. 11 We also pray

strengthened with all his glorious power so you will have all the endurance an

l. May you be filled with joy, 12 always thanking the Father. He has enabled you

nheritance that belongs to his people, who live in the light. 13 For he has rescu

rdom of darkness and transferred us into the Kingdom of his dear Son, 14 who pu

and forgave our sins. 15 Christ is the visible image of the invisible God. He ex

g was created and is supreme over all creation, 16 for through him God created e

eavenly realms and on earth. He made the things we can see and the things we c

thrones, kingdoms, rulers, and authorities in the unseen world. Everything was

him and for him. 17 He existed before anything else, and he holds all creation

s also the head of the church, which is his body. He is the beginning, supreme o

m the dead. So he is first in everything. 19 For God in all his fullness was plea

t, 20 and through him God reconciled everything to himself. He made peace with

n and on earth by means of Christ's blood on the cross. 21 This includes you who

from God. You were his enemies, separated from him by your evil thoughts and

w he has reconciled you to himself through the death of Christ in his physica

, he has brought you into his own presence, and you are holy and blameless as y

im without a single fault. 23 But you must continue to believe this truth and s

n't drift away from the assurance you received when you heard the Good News. T

s been preached all over the world, and I, Paul, have been appointed as God's se

d it. 24 I am glad when I suffer for you in my body, for I am participating in the

t that continue for his body, the church. 25 God has given me the responsibility

ch by proclaiming his entire message to you. 26 This message was kept secret f

erations past, but now it has been revealed to God's people. 27 For God wanted t

riches and glory of Christ are for you Gentiles, too. And this is the

Contents

we give thanks to God, the Father of our Lord Jesus Christ. 4 For we have heard
Christ Jesus and your love for all of God's people, 5 which come from your confi
God has reserved for you in heaven. You have had this expectation ever since yo
he truth of the Good News. 6 This same Good News that came to you is going out al
t is bearing fruit everywhere by changing lives, just as it changed your lives f
t heard and understood the truth about God's wonderful grace. 7 You learned ab
om Epaphras, our beloved co-worker. He is Christ's faithful servant, and he is h
behalf. 8 He has told us about the love for others that the Holy Spirit has given
not stopped praying for you since we first heard about you. We ask God to give y
ge of his will and to give you spiritual wisdom and understanding. 10 Then the
l always honor and please the Lord, and your lives will produce every kind of g
while, you will grow as you learn to know God better and better. 11 We also pray
strengthened with all his glorious power so you will have all the endurance an
d. May you be filled with joy, 12 always thanking the Father. He has enabled you
nheritance that belongs to his people, who live in the light. 13 For he has rescu
rdom of darkness and transferred us into the Kingdom of his dear Son, 14 who pu
and forgave our sins. 15 Christ is the visible image of the invisible God. He ex
g was created and is supreme over all creation, 16 for through him God created e
eavenly realms and on earth. He made the things we can see and the things we c
thrones, kingdoms, rulers, and authorities in the unseen world. Everything was
him and for him. 17 He existed before anything else, and he holds all creation
s also the head of the church, which is his body. He is the beginning, supreme o
m the dead. So he is first in everything. 19 For God in all his fullness was ple
st, 20 and through him God reconciled everything to himself. He made peace wit
en and on earth by means of Christ's blood on the cross. 21 This includes you wh
from God. You were his enemies, separated from him by your evil thoughts and
ow he has reconciled you to himself through the death of Christ in his physica
, he has brought you into his own presence, and you are holy and blameless as y
im without a single fault. 23 But you must continue to believe this truth and s
n't drift away from the assurance you received when you heard the Good News.
s been preached all over the world, and I, Paul, have been appointed as God's se
n it. 24 I am glad when I suffer for you in my body, for I am participating in the
t that continue for his body, the church. 25 God has given me the responsibilit
rch by proclaiming his entire message to you. 26 This message was kept secret f
erations past, but now it has been revealed to God's people. 27 For God wanted t

Introduction

HI, DEAR FRIEND!

I'd like to invite you to join me for a walk in small-town America! Though I grew up in Thailand as the child of Bible translators and I spent much of my early life attending an international school in Chiang Mai, my married life took me to a small rural community in southern New Hampshire. Our tiny town was settled amid the trees as opposed to wide-open farmland. We have a Walmart and one four-way traffic light, and our home sits on a hill overlooking a lake that my husband's father *dug* out. That's right, he dug his own lake with an excavator. My own father grew up in a nearby town, so there is a lot of family history here. My husband grew up on the same road we now live on, and his mom lives just down the street in a cabin that became a house over time during my husband's childhood. Life moves slowly here, and many of my friends raise goats and chickens and tend small hobby gardens. (I make no claims that I also raise goats and chickens or have a garden!)

My husband has always loved living in this small town in the midst of God's beautiful creation. He grew up four-wheeling and enjoying the great outdoors. Our kids practically live outside—they love fishing, biking, and exploring. When I talk about small-town life, I also mean it is small in the sense that we know so many of the people who live here. When we go out and about, we run into multiple people we know. A trip to the grocery store or the coffee shop means I'll have opportunities to smile, wave, or catch up on life.

I remember one afternoon, my husband and I jumped into our car to go somewhere, and I was driving. Instead of waiting at the four-way intersection with the stoplight, I took a shortcut to avoid the delay of the light. My husband couldn't believe I would take the shorter route. "By taking the shortcut, you miss seeing everyone and waving at them. I love going the way with the stoplight because you get to wave to your friends!" I could not stop laughing at this honest reason why my husband preferred to go through the stoplight. To him, having the opportunity to wave at his friends in the other vehicles brought him joy. If that doesn't scream small-town extrovert, I do not know what does!

Inductive Bible Study, like the slow route through the stoplight, is a slowed-down method of studying the Scriptures. Instead of hurriedly reading through a passage, a person using this method takes the time to observe the landscape, learn about the history and culture, and arrive at the message God was giving the original audience. You might even smile or have an imaginary conversation with a few characters while waiting. There is no real rush to get to the end. Instead you take in the journey, staying awhile and seeing what the Lord desires you to learn from the passages you study. As you sit with the text, you will see it come alive with deep meaning.

I first fell in love with the Inductive Bible Study method when I attended Bible college. As someone who grew up in a Christian household and thought I knew everything about studying the Bible, I was shocked when I felt like I was drinking from a fire hose of biblical knowledge. I later went on to create Chasing Sacred, an entire ministry based on this step-by-step method of studying Scripture. The journal we developed that teaches how to study the Bible using this method became wildly successful, and now I have made it my mission to teach the Inductive Bible Study method wherever I go! I wrote this study of Colossians and Philemon as a companion to my book *Chasing Sacred*. It's designed to help you take what you learned in the book and put Inductive Bible Study into practice.

Colossians is a letter Paul wrote to the church in Colossae, historically known as a small, unimportant city near Laodicea, similar to the small town I live in. Yet this book deals with *huge* theological themes and some of the most important Christ-centered topics in the New Testament.

Philemon is a personal letter from Paul to his friend Philemon, a wealthy businessman. Paul urges Philemon to forgive Onesimus, his runaway slave. Although this is one of the shortest letters in the Bible, it still packs a mighty punch!

Small-town gossip is no joke. Through the years of living in a small town, I have heard some very interesting stories. When I hear gossip, I go right to the source to ask if it is true. There is also a lot of hearsay about the Bible, unsubstantiated information that we have gathered from our presuppositions. (For more on this, see chapter 11 in my book *Chasing Sacred*.) These arise and inform our worldview as a result of the facts, experiences, people, and places we've encountered. Our worldview also includes things we have unknowingly come to believe due to our culture, upbringing, church traditions, or schooling. We must be willing to do the hard work of finding the truth and measuring our assumptions about the Bible against what the Bible actually says. That's where Inductive Bible Study comes in.

Inductive Bible Study is an approach to Scripture that uses a three-step process: observation, interpretation, and application. By taking these three steps, we will seek to discover the original intent of the author and what the author is saying to the original audience. Each week we will study a different chapter of Colossians or Philemon. We will begin with an introduction to the week, and then we will spend five days breaking down each passage using the inductive method. At the end of this study, my hope is that you will be able to take this method and apply it to any book of the Bible, walking into studying and teaching Scripture with a newfound confidence!

Getting Started

As we approach this study of Colossians and Philemon through the Inductive Bible Study method, we will learn to ask questions of the text. These questions are designed to help us discover what the specific passage is about and what the author's original intent was. Bible students love to call these the *W* and *H* questions.

We will ask those questions and more:

- Who was the author?
- Who was the audience?
- Who were the key characters in this passage?
- Why was it written?
- Where did it take place?
- How will it happen?
- What was the author saying?

I need someone to walk me through something before I actually understand it. (Maybe you can relate.) That's what I am hoping we can do as we chase sacred through the books of Colossians and Philemon together. As we learn how to do the Inductive Bible Study method, we will be following this three-step process:

Observation: "What do I see?" or "What does this say?"
Interpretation: "What does this mean?"
Application: "How does this apply to me?"

When we consider Scripture in context, we are like arrows aimed at the bull's-eye—the heart of the passage. To nail the correct interpretation of a verse or passage, we must hit the bull's-eye in light of the knowledge of the surrounding rings. Understanding the surrounding rings helps us to understand the main point of the passage. The outside ring represents the entirety of the Bible, the next ring represents the book that the verse is in, and the next one represents the specific passage of Scripture it is from. Our ultimate aim is to understand the heart of the passage. I want us to aim at the heart of God's message, seeking the purpose and meaning of God's Word while knowing that the surrounding rings matter.

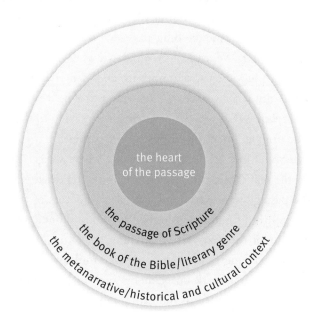

Before we dive into Inductive Bible Study, please pray with me that the Lord will provide His wisdom for this process.

Lord God,

I am so thankful for Your Word. As I begin studying Colossians and Philemon, I pray that You would enlighten my heart and show me Your truth. May You help me to hear, concentrate, and understand. Give me patience and endurance to see what is in the text. May I discover what You want to say to me through the pages of Scripture.

In Jesus' name, amen.

Observation

The first step in the Inductive Bible Study Method is observation. Observation asks the questions "What does this say?" and "What do I see?" We want to get to the bottom of what was truly happening with the original audience at the time the Bible passage was written, and we do this by examining the text. We read and write down what exactly is there. We withhold our own judgments, assumptions, and ideas about the text and just clearly identify what we see. We use our senses as we take notice of what God is saying. What was the original author saying to the audience? What was the original intent or purpose of the passage?

The Inductive Bible Study method is one where we get to see what is already in the text! We do this by observing the repeated words or key words in the passage we are studying. We also take note of any cultural, historical, or political figures mentioned. We can find out a lot by simply asking questions of the text. The first thing we do in the observation process is to read through the book or passage multiple times. Then we underline, highlight, or mark up elements such as key words, repeated words, and linking words; words indicating mood or tone; and historical and cultural observations.

If you are looking for further help for your study, you can check out my book *Chasing Sacred* (especially chapter 8 and the appendix) to find suggested resources.

Mark Key Words, Repeated Words, and Linking Words

During the observation stage, I will ask you to note or mark up any key words and repeated words in the passage you are reading. Noticing key-words is the first step to unlocking the meaning of the text. Key words are so important that, if they're taken out of the text, we lose the meaning of the sentence or the point of the passage. Repeated words are any words that are used over and over. I love to color-code, or highlight, these words. This helps them jump out at me. I have included a simplified guide to color-coding on page 124 of *Chasing Sacred*. We also want to pay close attention to linking words, which include *because, therefore, as if, but,* among others. They are transitional words that clue us into the meaning of the text.

For example, throughout the book of Colossians, look for references to *he, him, through him, in him,* etc. Look for repetition of the phrase "see to it," and in chapter 2, look for repetition of "let no one."

Compare Translations

Comparing translations shows us the various legitimate ways passages have been interpreted by different translators. It gives us a more comprehensive understanding of the passage and helps us to glean a well-rounded perspective on the original intent. Since my parents are Bible translators, I have a lot of thoughts on how to evaluate the strengths of different translations and understand the philosophies behind them. If you are interested in learning more about Bible translation and the variety of translation philosophies available, read chapter 7 of *Chasing Sacred.*

Define Unfamiliar Terms

When I come across a word I don't understand, I seek to define it right away. Once I understand the word, it shines light on the passage as a whole. Every word is important when it comes to understanding the meaning or purpose behind the passage.

Observe Historical, Cultural, and Political References

We will look into the passage's historical, cultural, and political references. By diving into the original setting and context, we will learn more about the original intent of the author. What was it like in the city of Colossae when Paul wrote his letter? What was the political situation? Who was Paul doing ministry with at the time?

Consider the Tone or Mood

Noting the atmosphere is a great way to see how biblical writers (in this case, Paul) felt when they thought about their audience. In Colossians, for instance, does Paul display a joyful tone like he does in the book of Philippians? Does he seem frustrated or worried about false teaching? Is he aiming to build up the church?

Again, observation asks the questions: "What does this say?" and "What do I see?" The steps listed above help us answer those questions as thoroughly as possible.

Interpretation

Interpretation is the next step in the Inductive Bible Study process, and I will lead you through it by providing commentary on each passage this study covers. Interpretation is how we come to understand what we are reading. It takes what we have observed about the text and asks the question "What does this mean?" God's revelation, written in God's way, still allows room for human responsibility. While interpreting, we draw conclusions on the themes we see. We must be sure to pay attention to the literary genre as well. Is it historical, narrative, poetry, wisdom literature? In the interpretation stage, we confirm what we are learning with commentaries and other resources.

When we interpret Scripture, we ask questions, including the following:

- Why did the author include this in the text?
- Why was it written?
- Why did the author say it in this way?
- Why did the original audience need to hear this?
- How is this going to happen?

For example: if you had never seen a refrigerator before and you walked into a room that had one, the first thing you might do is observe it. Then you might look inside it and try to figure out what it is useful for. What purpose does it have?

I remember helping my parents resettle refugees when I was fifteen. We spent a lot of our free time volunteering. One refugee lady had never used a fridge before. She had never owned a fridge or stored food in that way, so she did not have any context for its purpose. Once she learned what it was for, she moved her perishable items from the cupboard to the fridge. Similarly, when we observe and *see* something in the Scriptures, we need to take the next step to figure out why it is there. Sometimes we do not have the cultural bearings to understand why it was included. In the interpretation process, we follow cross-references to try to understand why the author uses the words and phrases that he does.

At this stage, we also want to draw meaning from what we have read by looking up words, people, and places that we have observed to learn their significance. We want to look up key words in their original language (Greek or Hebrew). We want to see if there is anything we do not understand. This all moves us toward finding the purpose of the passage.

Application

I walked into church the other day and scanned the room. I quickly took note of the fact that most families sit in the same seats every single Sunday. Yup, there were the Browns on the right, the Robertses on the left, and the Ahos in their usual spot too. There's nothing wrong with choosing the same pew every Sunday. But this got me thinking about how application requires us to change and move. It requires us to put something we learn into practice. So many times we sit in the same spot day after day, year after year—comfortable to sit underneath teaching but never actually change. Application is reading the Bible and then taking action. It is moving seats, taking risks, and letting the Holy Spirit change us from the inside out.

What do we indulge in when things are not going our way? Where do we turn with our frustrations? How do we act when our desires get thwarted? What do we find security in when we feel insecure? Application is our direct course of action or heart change after we read the pages of Scripture. We will learn to ask, *What is this passage teaching me, and how can I implement it in my life?* By God's grace, we can respond to the way the Holy Spirit prompts our heart and change.

I have spent most of my life with a PhD in applying the Bible to myself. It is *so* easy for me to use the pages of Scripture for myself. I can usually figure out how they relate to me or show me how I should change, and that's not a bad thing! The problem is when that's all I see in the passages I read.

Often, when we approach the Bible, we jump to application first and forget to do the first two steps of the Inductive Bible Study process. In Inductive Bible Study, the application is the last step because reading the Bible is not just about us. It also includes our brothers and sisters in Christ. Is God calling us to change the way we interact with others? Or is the passage primarily teaching us something about God's character? In and through the pages of Scripture, we learn so much about the character of God, and part of application is growing in our knowledge of who He is.

Before We Begin

Now that we have a basic background on the Inductive Bible Study method, let's get ready to put it into practice as we dive into the books of Colossians and Philemon. Many scholars believe that both Colossians and Philemon were written around the same time. The messages in both books are closely linked and tie together effortlessly. Our first step is pretty straightforward: read through the books of Colossians and Philemon front to back!

Let's answer our background questions on the book of Colossians. (Bible study resources are available in the appendices of this guide and my book *Chasing Sacred*.) We've already established the answers for the first three questions, and we're going to ask some additional questions specific to Colossians.

- Which book am I studying? (Colossians)
- Who wrote the book? (Paul)
- To whom was it written? (the Colossians)
- Where was it written?
- When was it written?
- What is the genre?

Where was Colossae?

The book of Colossians is a reflection of an actual time in history. Colossae was a real city located on a trade route in the area known today as Turkey. It was known for a specific type of purple-dyed wool. Colossae was the sister city to both Laodicea and Ephesus. The city of Colossae was destroyed by an earthquake at some point and never rebuilt. The book of Colossians would have been written in the last few years of Paul's earthly life when he was under house arrest. Paul never visited this city, so it is important to see how he begins and closes his letter with a focus on his apostolic authority.

> Colossae was a major city situated near the Meander River in the Lycus Valley.... Because of its commercial interests, Colossae had been a significant cosmopolitan city that included diverse religious and cultural elements.... By the time of the Apostle Paul, it was the least important city in the area. Historians record that it was severely devastated by an earthquake in AD 61, and unlike its neighboring cities of Laodicea (about ten miles west) and Hierapolis (about sixteen miles northwest), it was never rebuilt. The site was completely abandoned by the eighth century AD, and to this day no major archaeological work has been carried out on its ruins.[1]

Bonus: Find a map and locate where Colossae would have been. You can use a book like the *Rose Book of Bible Charts, Maps, and Time Lines* or look at a map in your study Bible.

When was the book written?

This book was written by Paul when he was in prison around AD 60–61.[2] Scholars have debated whether he was in Rome, or if it was during a different imprisonment. He had visitors when he was under house arrest, and he sent out letters while he was in Rome for two years. He probably wrote this letter around the time he wrote Philippians, Ephesians, and Philemon.

What was the false teaching going on in Colossae?

In every letter of Paul's, reconstructing the situation and learning as much as we can about what motivated the letter helps us piece together the reason for Paul's communication to the church. In chapter 2 of Colossians, for example, Paul tells the church that he hopes they will not be swayed by "fine-sounding arguments" (Colossians 2:4). What we know about this false teaching in Colossae was that it was similar to or had components of Gnosticism, a belief system that promoted hidden information or secret knowledge that was not available to most people. But the teaching seems to have contained other falsehoods as well. Some members of the Colossian church were combining pagan philosophies with Christianity. Paul was contending for the faith by teaching sound doctrine and reminding the believers that Christ is sufficient and supreme. We would do well to pay attention to how Paul counteracted this false heresy: he reminded the believers of Christ's supremacy.

Themes in the book of Colossians

Quite a few themes work their way through the book of Colossians, and they are encouraging when we can remember them during our daily struggles. These themes are *so* applicable to our everyday life, and if we can internalize them, we will have weapons to fight off feelings of insecurity, frustration, and jealousy.

Christ is God: All authority and dominion belong to Him. The book of Colossians clearly points to the fact that Christ is God. He is equal with the Father and the Holy Spirit. Because He is God, we need to make sure He is number one in our lives. Christ has all authority and power, which means we can rest knowing nothing is out of His hands. We do not need to strive for importance, to be seen, or to be heard, because He sees us, He hears us, and He is sovereign over our lives. The result of knowing that Christ is God is that we learn to submit to Him in all areas of our lives. We actively seek to trust Him with our concerns and the things we do not understand.

Christ is Creator: The book of Colossians tells us that "through [Christ] God created everything in the heavenly realms and on earth. He made the things we can see and the things we can't see—such as thrones, kingdoms, rulers, and authorities in the unseen world. Everything was created through him and for him" (1:16, NLT). The beginning is His, the end is His, the sum of our lives is His, and because of this, we can trust Him with everything. He is the One who creates a new, clean heart in us. All the frustrations, relational drama, and heartache will be redeemed in His time, in His way, and by His Word. I love this quote often attributed to Martin Luther: "The Christian shoemaker does his duty not by putting little crosses on the shoes, but by making good shoes, because God is interested in good craftsmanship."[3] Through Christ, God has created a world that we get to steward. Christ as Creator means He also sustains life, death, and growth. We grow up into fullness because of Him. As we encounter Him and let the Holy Spirit lead, we grow into Christlikeness and maturity. Also, after we have tasted and seen that the Lord is good, our appetite for Him should grow.

Union with Christ: Pastor and theologian Kevin DeYoung made this observation: "Union with Christ may be the most important doctrine you've never heard of."[4] The reality of our union with Christ—the idea that we exist in Him, and that He dwells in us—is everywhere in the book of Colossians. Because of what Christ did for us on the cross, it is possible to be united with Him and find our identity in Him. We become united with Christ when we believe in Him and the Holy Spirit dwells inside us.

Salvation in Christ: I found a beautiful, old-looking book hollowed out inside, and now I use it to hide my TV remote. Compared to all the gorgeous home decor I'd seen on Instagram, my TV remote looked like an eyesore. But it is now hidden in an attractive disguise. In a similar way, we as believers are now hidden in Christ. Colossians 1:14 says that Christ is the One "in whom we have redemption, the forgiveness of sins." When we trust in Him for salvation, Christ cloaks us in His righteousness. He took our place as the ultimate offering for our sins.

Christ's sufficiency: Sufficient means "enough" or "adequate." Many of us spend all our lives trying to fill the void that says, "You are not enough," and we search and search for that missing something. But Christ's sufficiency points to the fact that we are complete in Him. Again and again, Christ points us to His wisdom and knowledge (see Colossians 2:2-4). Feel confused about your direction in life? Not sure what to do next with your business or your family? He has all the knowledge and wisdom. When things go wrong in our lives and we lose what we feel like is our identity, we immediately start trying to find security. We start grasping for money, recognition at work, or affirmation from people. But the reality is that Christ is sufficient for us and for today's struggles. By God's grace, we can find hope and strength to meet today's challenges. He is also sufficient as the atonement for sin—no works from us are needed.

Christ's supremacy: In Thailand, where I grew up, every time the national anthem was played at the movie theater, we stood in respect of the king. In America, we stand and put our hands over our hearts to show respect for our flag. We go to sports games and scream and yell for our favorite team. These cultural actions depict respect and admiration. If Christ is supreme, we should be His biggest fans. Dictionary.com defines *supreme* as "highest in rank or authority; paramount; sovereign; chief." Colossians has a lot of verbiage that shows us Christ is God. He is over all things, which means He is worthy of our worship, and this should lead us to set our desires on Him as the sustainer of life. Every breath we breathe is from God. We walk in brotherly affection, desire good for people, and love others because of God. In times of animosity, we only find restraint because the power of the Spirit of God lives in us.

Chaos and order: The passages in chapter 1 of Colossians point to Christ's complete control over the cosmos. He is not surprised by the chaos that ensues, and it is not beyond His authority. When your anxious thoughts spin out of control, think about Christ. When you are facing a financial battle, think about Christ. When you feel insecure and want to make up for it by striving at work or in your home life, think about Christ. For every problem, Christ is the only remedy. For every anxious thought on earth, Christ above us. For every dashed desire, Christ over us. For every weary and tired heart, Christ within us, strengthening and upholding us. Stand in these truths.

I do not think it is an accident that God repeatedly calms the chaos and restores order in the Bible. The point is not so much about order and chaos in and of themselves but more about who controls the chaos and restores order. When I began writing this book, my friend asked me, "Is chaos bad?" Chaos forces us to rely on Christ in petition, prayer, and Bible reading. Although sin wreaks havoc and has horrible consequences, the conviction of sin pushes us toward a prayerful life. Pushes us to acknowledge the true King of His Kingdom.

Final Thoughts

Here are some items that will help you as you go through this study:

- A pen or pencil to fill out this workbook. Colored pencils are helpful for marking up the text.
- A physical Bible. It can be hard to use a phone because it's not possible to see as much of the text on the screen of your phone, and it's harder to take notes. I want you to get used to reading through the entire chapter of Scripture before you begin studying a specific focus verse. It's also easier to get distracted when you read the Bible on your phone.
- A commentary or two (Bible Hub and Blue Letter Bible are free online resources to help you get started). See the appendix in *Chasing Sacred* for how to use these websites, as well as some additional suggested resources.
- My book *Chasing Sacred*. This book explains all the ins and outs of Inductive Bible Study and includes more of my story too!

My heartfelt hope is that through this in-depth method of Bible study, you will take the time to learn about the places, people, and cultures of the

Bible and get to know God in a deeper, more intimate way, and that God's Word will forever impact your life. I cannot wait for you to join me in the pages ahead! Let's pray as we continue on this journey together.

Lord God,

We are so thankful for Your Word. As we begin studying Colossians, we pray that You would enlighten our hearts and show us Your truth. May You help us to hear, concentrate, and understand. Give us patience and endurance to hear and see what is in the text. May we discover what You want to say to us through the pages of Scripture.

In Jesus' name, amen.

Tips for Group Study

SO YOU AND YOUR FRIENDS or your Bible study group want to go through the book of Colossians with the Inductive Bible Study method? YES, ladies! Let's do it! This is a great study to do with your small group or church gathering. Here are a few suggestions on how to do this study as a group:

Week 1: Open in prayer. Meet together and discuss what you hope to learn from studying the book of Colossians. Read the book of Colossians together as a group, taking turns reading out loud. Read and discuss all the introductory pages of this study guide until you get to week 1 of the study. Ask if anyone has questions they would like to talk about or discuss during your time together. Close in prayer, and assign week one of this book for homework.

Week 2: Going day by day through week 1, read aloud the focus verses, then share with each other answers to the observation questions and discuss the interpretation sections for each day. Ask if anyone has questions about what you are learning. Discuss a few application questions from the week that you found particularly eye-opening or helpful. Ask if anyone would like to share from their personal reflection sections. Close in prayer, and assign week 2 of this book for homework.

Repeat the same format for the remaining weeks of the study.

Video Notes

Week 1: Colossians 1

_____

_____

_____

_____

_____

_____

_____

_____

_____

_____

_____

_____

_____

_____

_____

_____

_____

_____

*The Son is the image of the invisible God, the firstborn over all
creation. For in him all things were created: things in heaven and on
earth, visible and invisible, whether thrones or powers or rulers or
authorities; all things have been created through him and for him.
He is before all things, and in him all things hold together.*

COLOSSIANS 1:15-17

...we give thanks to God, the Father of our Lord Jesus Christ. 4 For we have hear...

...Christ Jesus and your love for all of God's people, 5 which come from your con...

...God has reserved for you in heaven. You have had this expectation ever since ...

...he truth of the Good News. 6 This same Good News that came to you is going out ...

...t is bearing fruit everywhere by changing lives, just as it changed your lives ...

...t heard and understood the truth about God's wonderful grace. 7 You learned a...

...om Epaphras, our beloved co-worker. He is Christ's faithful servant, and he is ...

...behalf. 8 He has told us about the love for others that the Holy Spirit has giv...

...not stopped praying for you since we first heard about you. We ask God to give ...

...ge of his will and to give you spiritual wisdom and understanding. 10 Then th...

...ll always honor and please the Lord, and your lives will produce every kind of ...

...while, you will grow as you learn to know God better and better. 11 We also pra...

...strengthened with all his glorious power so you will have all the endurance a...

...d. May you be filled with joy, 12 always thanking the Father. He has enabled yo...

...nheritance that belongs to his people, who live in the light. 13 For he has resc...

...rdom of darkness and transferred us into the Kingdom of his dear Son, 14 who p...

...a and forgave our sins. 15 Christ is the visible image of the invisible God. He e...

...g was created and is supreme over all creation, 16 for through him God created ...

...eavenly realms and on earth. He made the things we can see and the things we ...

...thrones, kingdoms, rulers, and authorities in the unseen world. Everything wa...

...n him and for him. 17 He existed before anything else, and he holds all creatio...

...s also the head of the church, which is his body. He is the beginning, supreme ...

...om the dead. So he is first in everything. 19 For God in all his fullness was pl...

...st, 20 and through him God reconciled everything to himself. He made peace wit...

...en and on earth by means of Christ's blood on the cross. 21 This includes you wh...

...y from God. You were his enemies, separated from him by your evil thoughts and ...

...ow he has reconciled you to himself through the death of Christ in his physica...

..., he has brought you into his own presence, and you are holy and blameless as ...

...im without a single fault. 23 But you must continue to believe this truth and ...

...on't drift away from the assurance you received when you heard the Good News. ...

...s been preached all over the world, and I, Paul, have been appointed as God's s...

...m it. 24 I am glad when I suffer for you in my body, for I am participating in the ...

...st that continue for his body, the church. 25 God has given me the responsibilit...

...rch by proclaiming his entire message to you. 26 This message was kept secret ...

...erations past, but now it has been revealed to God's people. 27 For God wanted ...

WEEK 1
COLOSSIANS 1

I STILL REMEMBER WHEN I KICKED a noisy toy off the balcony of our house into the woods in the wee hours of the morning, around 4 a.m. The torture device would not turn off, and at 5 a.m. I could still hear the faint sound of the murdered toy haunting my soul. I was sleep-deprived, and my toe ended up throbbing for days. Limping around, I was too prideful to admit that my emotions might have gotten the best of me.

Motherhood opened a floodgate of wild emotions that matched the pinging of the toy and grated on my nerves every single day. The sleepless nights dragged on, the clock ticking at the same frequency as my nerve endings and sending signals to my brain letting me know that I would *never* sleep again. It was all pure chaos. It seemed that I could not find a matching sock to save my life, my dryer was never empty, and as the older three boys grew, my pantry was never full. In the midst of this chaotic life, I found out I was expecting another baby. That would be five babies in seven years, and all my mind and body craved was a semblance of order. I remember weeping on the bathroom floor as I eyed the piles of clothes from the group shower I had stuck all the kids in days earlier. The soapsuds had left foam residue on the floor in front of me. My husband peeled my lifeless body off the tile floor as he said over and over, "You are going to be okay. You always pull through, Mikella. You are going to be okay." But I was overwhelmed.

In another moment of chaos, the Lord began to settle in my heart that He is a God of order and that He is above our chaos and fills it with meaning. On this occasion, I engaged in a little brawl—the kind of brawl a husband and wife get into when they do not see eye to eye. My husband, Jamie, yelled, "God is a God of order. Can you please take this task of organization seriously?!" It had been months and months where I felt like I was burning dinner, living in overwhelm, and haphazardly putting things in my kitchen cabinets so that something often hit our heads when we opened the doors. Jamie, whom God made to love order, was panicking at the unsightly mess that he and I found ourselves in.

Now, if you know me, you know I need theology to back any argument. The dishes were piled high, the house was a mess, and the children were wrestling. So my husband's frustrations received a pause of consideration before my rebellious nature yelled back, "Don't you dare bring *God* into this!" Yet it sparked my thinking, and I ferociously began to research if God truly was a God of order. What pleasantly surprised me in my study was how God's Word is so closely linked to the bringing about of order in the world. His Word created order at the very beginning of Creation. It was the Word, Jesus, who sacrificed Himself for us to bring our relationship with God back into order after the Fall. It is Scripture, God's Word, by which the power of the Holy Spirit works in us, clarifies who God is and who we are as His children, and draws us to loving, peaceful, ordered relationships with others. Knowing what God says fills the void of a purposeless, chaotic life. When life does not happen the way you plan, knowing that the Bible is a light to guide you home is everything. It is the order that I seek to cling to in my day-to-day life. Reading God's Word, knowing Him intimately, and obeying Him are the tools given to us to combat the disorder that sin brings.

The first chapter of Colossians is concerned with God's rightful order. God is the Creator of the world who established the world. He is sovereign over the chaos and disorder that we can and can't see—in both the created world and the supernatural realm. There is no entity that has power or dominion over Him. Paul uses this book to combat false teaching in the church of Colossae. He does this by demonstrating that Christ is the preeminent One, the One who is sufficient for all our needs. It is so easy to devalue the role of Christ in our lives, but when we read through Colossians, we will be convinced Christ is supreme. He should be our aim. We want to know more of Him and to give ourselves over to His agenda, refusing to be sidetracked by lesser concerns.

The richness of doctrine that surrounds these truths about Christ is paramount. He is supreme over all of creation and the cosmos, and we should acknowledge His rightful place in our lives. In this first chapter of Colossians, we find that He is "the firstborn of all creation" (verse 15, ESV) and has dominion over all authorities (has established His rule and reign over the cosmos). We learn that in Him "all things hold together" (verse 17), meaning that He is the One who keeps order in the universe. Life might feel chaotic, but Christ created all things and is before all things. He rules over the chaos. In the beautiful book of Colossians, we will observe how Christ is the answer to anything and everything we experience in life, even the chaos.

Focus Verses

Colossians 1:1-8

Observation

1. How does Paul introduce himself in this passage? (Remember to mark up any repeated words or key words as you answer this question.) Define *apostle*.

_____

_____

_____

2. Who was Timothy? Read Acts 16:1-3 and Philippians 2:20-22 to find out more about Timothy and his relationship with Paul. (As you read these passages, take note of the main characters and any historical, cultural, or geographical references.)

_____

_____

_____

Interpretation

Verses 1-3: This Epistle is endorsed by both Paul and Timothy. The concerns within it are shared concerns. Did you know that Paul mentions Timothy in eight of his letters, not including the two letters *to* Timothy? This shows us what a close companion and coworker Timothy was to Paul. Paul begins this letter by documenting his apostolic authority because he had not visited Colossae and needed to establish that his words were worth heeding. Paul's audience—the church of Colossae—was made up of both Jewish and Gentile Christians. Paul intentionally includes believers of both backgrounds by using salutations that were customary for each: grace (Gentiles) and peace (Jews). He establishes right away that he prays and thanks God for these believers. They are held in high esteem in Paul's mind even though he probably had never met them.

Verses 4-6: After Paul introduces himself, he includes information about what he has heard about the faith of the Colossian Christians. He has heard how they have been living out the Good News, the same Good News that is changing lives all around the world. An authentic, genuine faith is displayed in an individual's outpouring of love and kindness. If you are searching for evidence of a person's faith, look no further than the love he or she shows for other people. Here, Paul distinctively explains that real faith is shown by one's love.

Verses 7-8: In these verses, Paul introduces us to Epaphras, who is described as a servant and a faithful minister. Later in the book Paul says Epaphras is "always wrestling in prayer" (4:12). Epaphras has brought news to Paul of heresy being mixed into foundational doctrine in the church of Colossae. As one commentary says, "Paul devoted significant space to a discussion of Epaphras, who had taken the gospel to the Colossians (1:7-8). Epaphras worked closely with Paul and was most likely the founder of the Colossian church. . . . Thus, the gospel message advances through the world calling persons to Christ, communicating the message of grace, and being entrusted to the servants of Christ like Epaphras who proclaim it."[1]

Love comes from the Holy Spirit, and Paul heard of the Spirit's work in the Colossian believers' lives as demonstrated by their love for others. Paul reminds the believers in Colossae that changed lives are the result of Christ-centric gospel belief. Belief in Christ and submission to His lordship inevitably results in changed lives. He reminds the believers that God's grace and truth result in God's work in and through them.

Application

1. Have you personally observed someone's love for others that made you dwell on the Spirit's work in their life? What did that look like? This week, take the time to reach out to them and encourage them.

2. In this letter, Paul introduces himself as an apostle. How do you identify yourself in Christ? Who in God's family are you thankful for and why?

Space for Reflection

be strengthened with all his glorious power so you will have all the endurance
eed. May you be filled with joy, 12 always thanking the Father. He has enabled
e inheritance that belongs to his people, who live in the light. 13 For he has re
ingdom of darkness and transferred us into the Kingdom of his dear Son, 14 who
lom and forgave our sins. 15 Christ is the visible image of the invisible God. He
ning was created and is supreme over all creation. 16 for through him God create
e heavenly realms and on   e can see and the things w
as thrones, kingdoms, rul   unseen world. Everything
igh him and for him. 17 He   se, and he holds all creati
st is also the head of the   e is the beginning, suprem
from the dead. So he is first in everything. 19 For God in all his fullness was
rist, 20 and through him God reconciled everything to himself. He made peace w
aven and on earth by means of Christ's blood on the cross. 21 This includes you

Day Two

Focus Verses

Colossians 1:9-14

Observation

1. Mark up any references to *he*, *him*, *his*, *Spirit*, *God*, and *Father*.

2. In a study Bible or commentary (such as blueletterbible.org or biblehub.com), look up the definition of *worthy* in the phrase "worthy of the Lord" (verse 10). (Head to chapter 11 and the appendix in my book *Chasing Sacred* for more guidance on word studies.) What did you find? What is the Greek word here? Look up Ephesians 4:1 and Philippians 1:27, which include this same word. Compare the ways the word is used in these three verses.

_____

_____

_____

_____

_____

Interpretation

Verses 9-11: The fruit of a Christian's walk will be their conduct because Christian conduct should match a believer's profession of faith. When we mark up all the uses of *he, him, his, Spirit, God,* and *Father,* we see that Paul is emphasizing how our Christian faith should bear witness to the ways God graciously works out truths in our heart. Paul is urging the believers that correct knowledge leads to correct living. Paul continues to pray for the church that they be strengthened with power to live lives worthy of the Lord. "The main idea is that a Christian's *profession* is to correspond with his or her *confession.*"[2] His prayer for them is that they would be strengthened according to Jesus' glorious might so that they may have great endurance and patience. That is exactly what we need—endurance and patience while doing Kingdom work! Many of us get discouraged at how slow it feels we are growing, how slow others are growing, and how long it takes us to learn a lesson.

Verse 12: Not only does Paul pray that the Christians will have patience and endurance, but he also prays for joy. Paul is not praying for the believers to have success or to be profitable but instead to have hearts of joy and gratitude while they endure in the faith before God. How many of us in Christian ministry are praying for endurance, patience, joy, and thankfulness rather than numerical growth, success, and accolades?

Verses 13-14: Because of Jesus' death on the cross, we have received forgiveness for our sins and restoration to right order with Him. We now get to have a relationship with Jesus. We can know Him and let Him speak into our lives and relationships. We experience the love of Christ daily. We get to walk hand in hand with Him along life's path. Although we still live in a fallen world, He is the light in the darkness. The order to our chaos.

Sin fractures relationships, hurts spouses, estranges family members from each other, and creates unimaginable darkness. This chaos is also visible when we turn on the nightly news and see what sin does. What sin breaks. How innocent people in Myanmar are being gunned down by the

Burmese army. How women in Afghanistan are living with burdensome restrictions. When we observe the evil in politics or hear of an earthquake that killed hundreds of people, we are grieved. We are grieved when we hear about the horrific realities of sex trafficking or witness any other chaos that exists because of sin.

Today, we believers live in a mix of chaos and order. An already-but-not-yet reality. But throughout Scripture we see a restoration of order that will come to its fullness in Revelation. Until then, we can be thankful that we live in God's already-but-not-yet Kingdom. We experience some order now, but

> living east of Eden, as we do today, involves some chaos, disorder. This chaos is evil in that, as a result of sin, it involves pain, suffering, and death. But because of God's grace and faithfulness to his creation, there is still some order east of Eden: the succession of seasons and of day and night; the earth bringing forth vegetation; creatures thriving in the waters, the sky, and the earth; and human beings bearing children and finding food. Struggling for a living east of Eden is a mix of chaos and cosmos.[3]

Application

1. We can learn a lot when we look at different passages of the Bible and acknowledge their purpose. Are they a command, a prayer, an encouragement, or a teaching? Paul offers both thanksgiving (verse 12) and prayer (verse 9) in this passage. Today, take a section of this Scripture passage and pray it over someone in your life.

2. Read Ephesians 3:14-16. How does the power talked about in both Colossians and Ephesians encourage you in your daily living?

_____

_____

_____

3. One commentator explains the word *endurance* this way: "Endurance . . . is that lasting quality that enables one to continue toward a goal. . . . The Greek word *makrothymia*, often translated as 'patience' or 'long-suffering,' is that quality of self-restraint that enables a person to withstand opposition without retaliation."[4] In what ways is God calling you to have endurance and patience in your life right now?

_____

_____

_____

_____

Space for Reflection

_____

_____

_____

_____

_____

_____

_____

_____

_____

_____

_____

_____

_____

_____

_____

_____

Day Three

Focus Verses

Colossians 1:15-20

Observation

1. Read Genesis 1 to remind yourself of the context of the Bible as a whole, and then write down any similarities between Genesis 1 and this section of Colossians.

   _____

   _____

   _____

2. Make a list of the ways that Paul is establishing Christ's lordship and preeminence (superiority) in this passage. Write down everything Christ rules over, according to this passage.

   _____

   _____

   _____

Interpretation

Verse 15: This passage brings us right back to Genesis, the beginning of Creation. The focus is on Christ, through whom all things were made and who holds all things together. The order of the priorities in our lives should echo His authority. This is one of the strongest statements of Christ being God in the New Testament. Paul is telling the readers that Christ is fully, truly, and completely God.

Verse 16: The very beginning of Creation reveals something wild. Let's go back to Genesis to understand what Paul is referencing here when he refers to creation. Most readers skip right over the part that talks about the world being formless and void. Genesis 1:2 says that before God ordered the universe and called it good, He revealed the state of the world as disordered and empty: "Now the earth was formless and void, and darkness was over the surface of the deep. And the Spirit of God was hovering over the surface of the waters" (BSB). The Hebrew word for "formless" in this passage is *tohu*, which refers to chaos. Why would God reveal a chaotic void steeped in darkness? Everything God created is good, yet He shows the state of the world was chaotic and empty. Nothing God created was evil. However, other places that we observe the word *tohu* in Scripture depict a desert, a wilderness, purposelessness, chaos, confusion, and vanity. The Spirit of God is hovering over the chaos, ruling over the formlessness and the unknown waters. The Spirit hovering over these waters would have been significant to the ancient Israelites, who viewed the sea as unpredictable.

Verses 17-19: God's reign is distinct because He is without any rival. Without any battle, He brought order from chaos. Ancient Near Eastern creation myths mirror the Creation story in the Bible and yet have many differences. Right here from the beginning, we can observe why it is important to root ourselves in cultural context when studying the Word of God.

The Spirit of God hovering over the water shows us who rules the deep waters. One translation of Genesis 1:2 says, "The raging ocean that covered everything was engulfed in total darkness, and the Spirit of God was moving over the water" (GNT). To the Jews, the sea was daunting, powerful, and untamable. Yet when we see Jesus interacting with the sea in the Gospel accounts, He sleeps as a storm roars around Him, and at His command, the storm stops (see Matthew 8:24-26). He walks on top of the water and empowers Peter to do the same (see Matthew 14:25-32). When the Jews thought of the sea, they feared it, but God commands the sea, and the sea splits (see Exodus 14:21).

Your life might feel as chaotic and unordered as a raging sea, but the Spirit hovers over it. He fills it, and He orders it. Part of chasing sacred is learning to keep our eyes on Christ and to follow God even through the tumultuous seasons of life. Nothing will satisfy us or bring us comfort like Christ. The only true order comes from the Spirit's work and guidance in your life. He is sovereign over any confusion you are feeling. Now we know that this initial void and chaos was not inherently evil. God created and designed the world in an orderly manner. What disrupted that order, bringing in an evil chaos? Enter sin. The Fall happened when Adam and Eve disobeyed, and sin entered the picture for all humanity. Our sinful nature disturbed the order that God created.

In the Creation account, God pooled the water into one place; He created seasons and vegetation. He was precise about time and place and declared it good. How did God create this order? He created it by His Word. His powerful, light-revealing, life-giving Word brought rhythm, order, and goodness. Yet we know that God the Father was not alone at the very beginning of time. We know that the Spirit was hovering over the water, and here in this passage of Colossians, we learn that it was through Jesus that all things were created. The Gospel writer John affirms this reality when he echoes the Creation account: "In the beginning the Word already existed. The Word was with God, and the Word was God" (John 1:1, NLT).

Verse 20: Here we see that Christ reconciles all people and all things through his death on the cross. His death and resurrection make restored relationships possible. The truth is that your heart may have been broken by betrayal or deception. Or maybe you sinned against someone else. We all have reaped the consequences of sin in our world. When we reject the Word of God, we disobey God Himself. The opposite of order is a life ruled by sin, brokenness, and chaos. Sin creates rifts in our relationships, hurts the people we care about the most, and frustrates the peace we can experience in a relationship with God. Establishing right order in our lives means we order our lives around Christ and establish our priorities to reflect that. It means that those who have hurt us or betrayed us can be restored. It means we, who have betrayed God, can be restored too!

Application

1. What does it mean to you personally that God is a God of order who rules over the cosmos? When you think of the word *order*, what comes to mind?

   _____

   _____

   _____

2. Why do you think Paul would choose to include such a significant focus on Jesus' divinity in his letter?

   _____

   _____

   _____

3. Take some time to meditate on this powerful passage from Colossians. Here we see that Christ is the ruler, the authority over all of creation. How should the understanding of Christ's total sovereignty and rule over all things change the way we view our life circumstances?

   _____

   _____

   _____

Space for Reflection

_____
_____
_____
_____
_____
_____
_____
_____
_____
_____
_____
_____
_____
_____
_____
_____
_____
_____
_____
_____
_____
_____
_____
_____
_____

Day Four

Focus Verses

Colossians 1:21-23

These verses are a promise for God's people. To read more about promises from God in the Bible, turn to page 208 of Chasing Sacred.

Observation

1. Paraphrase this passage in your own words.

_____

_____

_____

_____

_____

_____

2. Highlight or list any linking (transitional) words in this passage, such as *by*, *because of*, *but now*, *if*, etc.

Interpretation

Verses 21-22: In this section, Paul shows us how God communicates clearly through Christ. God draws us into loving communion with Him, and when we begin to see that the whole Bible centers around the person of Christ, we also see how our lives are divided between before we knew Christ and after. A friend of mine told me that after her dad's death, she defined everything in her life by whether it happened before or after that moment. She would categorize photos in her head from times when she was happier and times after the tragedy when she was sad. Life meant something different before and after her father's passing. In so many ways, our lives should be marked in such a way that we find that everything is different once we know Christ.

Paul acknowledges that without Jesus' death on the cross—His substitutionary atonement—we would never be able to have a relationship with Him. Through Christ's work on our behalf, we have been declared blameless, set free from the laws of sin and death. These truths are more than sufficient for today's troubles. Even more so, the union we as believers share with Christ is more than sufficient for our past, present, and future sin, as well as our worries, anxieties, frustrations, and more.

Verse 23: God's Word is one of the ways He invites us into a relationship with Him, as Paul reminds us in this verse. His Word brings life, wisdom, and clarity. Abiding in His Word means we live as His disciples. We need to saturate ourselves in the Word in order to stand firm in it, and the pinnacle of the Word is Christ crucified. When we seek after God's Word, we are seeking after God Himself. Part of a life of chasing sacred is to chase His commands and chase His instruction for our lives. In order to continue to believe, we must regularly remind ourselves of the truth of His saving work on our behalf. We must pursue Christ as He pursues us by His grace!

Application

1. What does it mean to you that you were once far away from God but now He "has brought you into his own presence" (Colossians 1:22, NLT)? One of the most calming presences I have in my life is my mom. Similarly, when I am in close proximity to my children, I can calm their fears, hold their hands, and communicate that I love them. What does God's nearness communicate to you?

   _____

   _____

   _____

2. Think about your life before you knew Jesus versus your life since you came to know Him. How has it changed? What changes are still in process?

   _____

   _____

   _____

Space for Reflection

_____

_____

_____

_____

_____

_____

_____

Focus Verses

Colossians 1:24-29

Observation

1. What is the secret or mystery that Paul tells the church of Colossae?

   _____

   _____

2. How does this mystery provide comfort to you?

   _____

   _____

   _____

3. Mark or list any repeated words.

   _____

   _____

Interpretation

Verse 24: Paul reminds the Colossians that his ministry is one of suffering. He was writing to the church from house arrest.

Verses 25-28: Paul explains the ministry given to him to preach the Gospel. He shows the church of Colossae that all of the Bible centers around Christ: "We preach not fundamentally an ethical code or a set of doctrine or right behavior, but *Christ*."[5] This is the pinnacle of his message: "the glorious riches of this mystery, which is Christ in you, the hope of glory" (verse 27). As Elisabeth Elliot so famously states, "The secret is *Christ* in *me*, not me in a different set of circumstances."[6] The secret that Paul wants all believers to understand is that the secret is "Christ in you." Everyone is looking for peace and fulfillment. We all want to be satisfied and to lead purposeful, comfortable lives.

If you're a parent, you know it's easy to focus on external behavior modification with our kids. It is also easy for our own Christian walk to become externally motivated, whether we behave a certain way because people are watching or refrain from gossiping because of what people might think. But Paul continually points us toward our union with Christ, which is our only hope of glory. Paul reminds us that *this* is Christian ministry. It is not about success, numbers, or how many are watching. Instead, he roots us in what ministry looked like for him.

Verse 29: Paul's desire was not for numerical growth or billboard success, but for the inner strength that Christ provides. Paul toiled and struggled for the sake of the Colossian church.

Application

1. Paul talks of his suffering and striving on behalf of those he was doing ministry for. He worked hard to fight for others' hearts. In our culture, how do we measure a "successful ministry"? How is that different from what Paul describes?

2. What does Paul say is our "hope of glory"? What are some things you may have misplaced your hope of glory in? (As an example, I often look at my bank account to see what I'm spending money on. This helps me determine if I am misplacing my hope in material things or if my heart is sinking its security into places other than Jesus, whether my looks, ministry, or desire for success.)

Space for Reflection

Prayer

Friends, I cannot think of a more effective way to pray than to use the very Scriptures we are learning about to pray for ourselves or someone we love. (I have included some little changes to the passage to personalize these verses for us.)

Dear Lord,

Thank You so much for Your Word. I pray it continues to pierce my heart and speak to me in the ways You want it to. I pray for the endurance, patience, and joy that is talked about in these passages.

Lord God, I pray Colossians 1:9-14 over myself, and others:

We continually ask God to fill [us] with the knowledge of his will through all the wisdom and understanding that the Spirit gives, so that [we] may live a life worthy of the Lord and please him in every way: bearing fruit in every good work, growing in the knowledge of God, being strengthened with all power according to his glorious might so that [we] may have great endurance and patience, and giving joyful thanks to the Father, who has qualified [us] to share in the inheritance of his holy people in the kingdom of light. For he has rescued us from the dominion of darkness and brought us into the kingdom of the Son he loves, in whom we have redemption, the forgiveness of sins.

In Jesus' name, amen.

Final Thoughts

Video Notes

Week 2: Colossians 2

When you were dead in your sins and in the uncircumcision of your flesh, God made you alive with Christ. He forgave us all our sins, having canceled the charge of our legal indebtedness, which stood against us and condemned us; he has taken it away, nailing it to the cross. And having disarmed the powers and authorities, he made a public spectacle of them, triumphing over them by the cross.

COLOSSIANS 2:13-15

we give thanks to God, the Father of our Lord Jesus Christ. 4 For we have heard
Christ Jesus and your love for all of God's people, 5 which come from your confi
God has reserved for you in heaven. You have had this expectation ever since yo
he truth of the Good News. 6 This same Good News that came to you is going out a
t is bearing fruit everywhere by changing lives, just as it changed your lives f
t heard and understood the truth about God's wonderful grace. 7 You learned ab
om Epaphras, our beloved co-worker. He is Christ's faithful servant, and he is h
behalf. 8 He has told us about the love for others that the Holy Spirit has given
not stopped praying for you since we first heard about you. We ask God to give y
ge of his will and to give you spiritual wisdom and understanding. 10 Then the
l always honor and please the Lord, and your lives will produce every kind of g
while, you will grow as you learn to know God better and better. 11 We also pray
strengthened with all his glorious power so you will have all the endurance an
l. May you be filled with joy, 12 always thanking the Father. He has enabled you
nheritance that belongs to his people, who live in the light. 13 For he has resc
gdom of darkness and transferred us into the Kingdom of his dear Son, 14 who pu
and forgave our sins. 15 Christ is the visible image of the invisible God. He ex
g was created and is supreme over all creation, 16 for through him God created
eavenly realms and on earth. He made the things we can see and the things we c
thrones, kingdoms, rulers, and authorities in the unseen world. Everything wa
him and for him. 17 He existed before anything else, and he holds all creation
s also the head of the church, which is his body. He is the beginning, supreme
m the dead. So he is first in everything. 19 For God in all his fullness was ple
st, 20 and through him God reconciled everything to himself. He made peace wit
en and on earth by means of Christ's blood on the cross. 21 This includes you wh
from God. You were his enemies, separated from him by your evil thoughts and
ow he has reconciled you to himself through the death of Christ in his physica
, he has brought you into his own presence, and you are holy and blameless as
im without a single fault. 23 But you must continue to believe this truth and
n't drift away from the assurance you received when you heard the Good News.
s been preached all over the world, and I, Paul, have been appointed as God's s
m it. 24 I am glad when I suffer for you in my body, for I am participating in the
t that continue for his body, the church. 25 God has given me the responsibilit
rch by proclaiming his entire message to you. 26 This message was kept secret
erations past, but now it has been revealed to God's people. 27 For God wanted

MY SON'S TEACHER TAUGHT HIM that if you lined up all your blood vessels, you could wrap them around the earth more than twice. She also told him that a human being has around 206 bones in their body. When fact-checking this, I also discovered that if you stretched out your intestines, they would be as tall as a three-story house.[1] And ten thousand human cells can fit on the head of a pin! Talk about seeing all that the human body contains in a different light! The human body is truly astonishing. Yet, everything included in our bodies is essential for life (well, except for that appendix and our wisdom teeth!). As living, breathing organisms, we can eat, drink, and move our bodies. Many of us can walk to school or run a race. But we often take our bodies for granted. How often do we stop and think about how they automatically work, whether we're exercising or lying down to sleep at night? Similarly, we often take Christ's work on our behalf for granted.

In the book of Colossians, we learn about all the blessings and benefits contained and wrapped up in the person of Christ for those who are His: God became flesh, dwelled with us, and saved us from our sins. The gospel message emphasizes both the humanity and divinity of Christ: "In Christ all the fullness of the Deity lives in bodily form, and in Christ you have been brought to fullness. He is the head over every power and authority" (Colossians 2:9-10).

Over and over again, Paul talks about what is contained "in Christ" or "in him." All this "in him" talk points toward a biblical truth known as union with Christ. We die to our sinful flesh and come alive in righteousness. As believers, we are hidden in Him, and all knowledge and wisdom are hidden in Him as well. Paul writes of his desire that the church "may have the full riches of complete understanding, in order that they may know the mystery of God, namely, Christ, in whom are hidden all the treasures of wisdom and knowledge" (Colossians 2:2-3). Did you hear that? Everything we need for life and godliness is found in Him. Remarkable!

The gift of the gospel is that we are united with Christ. We discover that, like a Christmas morning surprise, underneath the work of Christ on our behalf is Christ Himself, who is sufficient for anything we are going through today. Whether we are battling insecurity, overwhelming circumstances, our stage of life, cancer, or another challenge, Paul teaches that fulfillment is found in Jesus. He is enough. The facts my son and I learned about the human body surprised me, as I hadn't realized the inside of my body had so many intricate details. Sometimes we need the reminder that there is so much more contained in the work of Christ than we can ever seek to wrap our minds around. Our righteousness is wrapped up in His resurrection. Because of His death, we were made alive in Christ. No plan of His can be thwarted because He rules the world.

The answers to all your most pressing life questions are in Christ. The strength you need to face tomorrow is in Christ. The power to overcome temptation is in Christ. In Christ, you are not lacking anything but instead have the full assurance that you can stand firm against temptation and false teaching.

Day One

Read all of Colossians 2.

Focus Verses

Colossians 2:1-5

Observation

1. What was Paul's goal? What did he want the church to know?

   _____

   _____

2. Highlight or make a list of all the occurrences of the words *in* and
   by and the words surrounding them. Note especially the phrase
   "deceive you by fine-sounding arguments" (verse 4).

   _____

   _____

Interpretation

Verses 1-2: Paul begins by talking about how hard he is "contending" for
the Christians in Colossae and Laodicea. Being a critic is much easier than
being a contender. Calling people out is much easier than calling people up.

Paul continually talks about how he strives on behalf of the church—and that his goal is for the church to be encouraged and united in love. Imagine if Christians today struggled and contended for others in the way Paul does here. How would the church be different?

God's power and wisdom are sufficient for all of our doubts, fears, and dashed hopes. When you have the assurance of Christ's worthiness, you are at peace with how He works. Paul is making a "dig" here at the Gnostic heresy with the phrase "know the mystery of God." The Gnostics wanted secret knowledge, but what they were truly after is contained in the work of Christ and who He is.

Verses 3-4: Here Paul describes where true wisdom and knowledge come from: Christ. Then he contrasts the knowledge and wisdom we find in Christ with the world's wisdom. Warning the Colossians against deception, Paul reminds them that these false teachings actually do sound like "fine-sounding arguments" (verse 4). Often, false teaching does not sound stupid; instead it is usually quite persuasive. That is why it is so important to stand on guard.

Verse 5: Paul's hope for those hearing this letter was that they would continue in their firm, disciplined faith in Christ. If they are to see how Christ unites them in love (see verse 2), then Christ must be primary. Although Paul is not directly with the believers, he is still with them because he is contending for them in prayer and in support.

Application

1. How could having "full riches of complete understanding" (verse 2) of Christ's love and knowledge bring peace to a situation you are facing right now? If you feel you are lacking assurance, ask God to bring your heart and mind to greater understanding of His character.

_____

_____

_____

2. Paul talks about three mysteries or secrets in Colossians 1 and 2:

> The church, as the body of Christ
> Our hope of glory, which is Christ in us
> Jesus as the One who guides us in wisdom[2]

Which one speaks to you the most? How could understanding these three mysteries change how you live?

_____

_____

_____

Space for Reflection

_____

_____

_____

_____

_____

_____

_____

_____

_____

_____

_____

_____

_____

Focus Verses

Colossians 2:6-8

This is a prescriptive passage of Scripture. To read more about prescriptive passages, turn to page 53 of Chasing Sacred.

Observation

1. Mark or list any verbs you see in this passage of Scripture.

   _____

   _____

   _____

2. Read Colossians 1:12 and Colossians 3:17. What do these verses have in common with Colossians 2:7?

   _____

   _____

   _____

   _____

Interpretation

Verse 6: At the very beginning of our Christian walk, we have simple faith. To come to know Christ as our risen Savior and Lord of our life, we simply need to receive His work on our behalf, trust, repent, and believe. Salvation comes by grace through faith (see Ephesians 2:8-9). False teachers often over-complicate this, but Paul brings us back to the understanding that we must walk in simple faith. We do not need any additions to our faith in Christ.

Verse 7: As Christians, we are to be known by our thankfulness. Not our worries, stresses, divisions, frustrations, or constant grumbling—but our thankfulness. We must trust God with the outcome of our lives and stay rooted in the things we were taught with thanksgiving. Paul continues to show us the importance of being "in him" (in Christ). We tend to worry about so many other things. Let's make sure to stay grounded and rooted in what actually matters.

Verse 8: Human philosophies often add to Jesus. Jesus plus nothing is what Paul teaches. We see an overemphasis on human philosophies when certain signs and wonders are said to be necessary for salvation. We see this when we add any sort of New Age beliefs to Jesus or when we sink into legalism. We also see this when we begin to accept false teaching that says we will be blessed materially and endure no hardship if we truly have faith.

One year on April Fools', my son put some barbecue sauce in our shampoo bottle. I thought it was hilarious! I used the shampoo and had no idea I was pouring barbecue sauce into my hair. The white overtook the brown, so it was hard to see that there was anything but shampoo in the bottle. I meant to throw the bottle away because it was contaminated, but I ended up using it until it ran dry. The truth is, there wasn't enough sauce in there to cause alarm—and it was a brand-new bottle, so I didn't want to waste it. My husband and I continued to use it all up, even *with* the barbecue sauce in it.

When I read the book of Colossians, I am often surprised at how much love and respect Paul has for the Colossian church. Yet he is stern in his rebuke of the false teaching infiltrating the body of believers. This teaching includes elements of legalism, Gnosticism, worship of angels, and mysticism. A little barbecue sauce may not have harmed my shampoo, but any amount of false teaching can threaten our commitment to the core doctrines of our faith. We must stay vigilant, watchful, and awake—not apathetic.

Application

1. Colossians 2:7 encourages us to be "rooted and built up in him."
   What does this look like in your own Christian walk?

   _____

   _____

2. What are some hollow and deceptive philosophies you see in the culture around you right now? How can you safeguard your heart and mind against these false teachings?

   _____

   _____

Space for Reflection

_____
_____
_____
_____
_____
_____
_____
_____

Day Three

Focus Verses

Colossians 2:9-12

Observation

1. Mark or list all the instances of "in Christ," "in him," or "with him" in this passage.

2. Mark or list all the statements that contrast works of the flesh (the physical) with God's works (the spiritual).

Interpretation

Verses 9-10: The head coach of the Boston Celtics was interviewed in 2022 after a game that Prince William and Princess Kate had attended. The reporter asked the coach, "Did you get a chance to meet with the royal family?"

The head coach, who had just cleaned up the court with his team, responded, "Jesus, Mary, and Joseph?"

The reporter clarified that she was referencing "the prince and princess of Wales."

The coach said, "Oh no, I did not. I'm only familiar with one royal family. I don't know too much about that one."[3]

As this story reminds us, God—the Father, Son, and Holy Spirit (the Trinity)—is "the head over every power and authority" (verse 10). There is no human authority who can compete with Christ's authority over creation. Paul urges the Colossian church not to be taken over by false teaching by reminding them of Christ's deity. Christ is supreme over all human authority and powers, and He is sufficient for salvation.

When the Holy Spirit lives inside us, we are given fullness of life. Christ is God—not a part of God, not some of God, but the *sum* of Christ *is God*. These verses emphasize Christ's deity, and that Jesus took on flesh dwelling among us. We often think we need more knowledge, power, or money to be happy and ensure our identity. But Christ is the ruler of every power and authority. He is enough.

Verse 11: Circumcision was a sign of the covenant between God and Israel. This verse shows us that physical circumcision was intended to represent spiritual circumcision. When we make the choice to follow Christ, our old sinful nature is cut away, and we become new in Him. He changes our hearts, and the Holy Spirit dwells within us. Spiritual circumcision takes place when we follow Christ and He works in our hearts.

Verse 12: We marvel at human hands that sculpt statues. We are amazed at modern medicine that heals life-threatening diseases. We gasp at runners who complete ultramarathons and athletes who scale the heights of mountains and free dive into the depths of the sea. We are in awe when we enter the same room as the royal family or a celebrity, but do we truly see the importance of what Christ did for us on the Cross and who He is to us today?

Self-denial is common to all religions. Self-effort even more so. But neither self-effort nor self-denial gets us into God's Kingdom. We come to salvation through faith because of God's grace. As we walk in step with the Spirit, we are ruled by Christ. He works in us until that work has reached completion. The power for all this is through Him who raised Christ from the dead.

Application

1. What worry or circumstance in your life needs to be submitted to Christ's "power and authority" today?

2. What is something in your old life that Jesus has helped you put off—or something that He has helped you put on since starting your new life as a Christian?

Space for Reflection

Focus Verses

Colossians 2:13-15

This is a descriptive passage of Scripture. To read more about descriptive passages, turn to page 53 of Chasing Sacred.

Observation

1. Mark or list the promises this passage says are available to us through Christ's work on our behalf.

   _____

   _____

   _____

2. Look at the different metaphors Paul uses in this passage, such as the courtroom imagery (canceling the charge of our legal indebtedness, nailing our charge to the cross, and making a spectacle out of the powers and authorities). Use the chart below to list phrases from this passage. For example, under "Before

Christ," write, "dead in sins." Under "After Christ," write, "alive with Christ." Compare the lists.

BEFORE CHRIST	AFTER CHRIST

Interpretation

Verses 13-15: Paul explains the implications of a dead man becoming alive. In death, there is no hope, but in life there is always hope. We were dead in our sin and have been made alive in Christ. There is a complete reversal because of what Christ did. He forgave us of our sins, so now we can live righteous and holy lives. I love this explanation from David Guzik:

> A dead man feels comfortable in his coffin; but if he were to be made alive again, he would instantly feel suffocated and uncomfortable. There would be a strong urge to escape the coffin and leave it behind. In the same way, when we were spiritually dead we felt comfortable in trespasses and sins; but having come to new life we feel we must escape that coffin and leave it behind.[4]

Paul also shows us what Christ's death accomplished on our behalf. What did He achieve when He died for us?

Application

1. This passage describes several incredible things Christ has done on our behalf. Which of these are you most thankful for? Why?

_____

_____

_____

2. God is in the restoration business. Think about the great reversal of how the cross symbolized shame and Jesus was made to be a public spectacle. Then He triumphed over death and made a public spectacle of the rulers and authorities. He took what was meant for public shame and shamed His enemies. He took death and made us alive. Nothing is impossible for Him. Reflect on the reversal that Christ has accomplished in your own life.

_____

_____

_____

_____

Space for Reflection

_____

_____

_____

_____

_____

_____

_____

strengthened with all his glorious power so you will have all the endurance a
d. May you be filled with joy, 12 always thanking the Father. He has enabled yo
nheritance that belongs to his people, who live in the light. 13 For he has resc
gdom of darkness and transferred us into the Kingdom of his dear Son, 14 who pu
n and forgave our sins. 15 Christ is the visible image of the invisible God. He ex
ng was created and is supreme over all creation. 16 for through him God created
heavenly realms and on ear   n see and the things we
thrones, kingdoms, rulers,   een world. Everything wa
n him and for him. 17 He exi   and he holds all creation
is also the head of the chu   s the beginning, supreme
om the dead. So he is first in everything. 19 For God in all his fullness was ple
st, 20 and through him God reconciled everything to himself. He made peace wit
en and on earth by means of Christ's blood on the cross. 21 This includes you wh

Day Five

Focus Verses

Colossians 2:16-23

Observation

1. Mark up or list any repeated words or phrases that you see.

   _____

   _____

   _____

2. List everything Paul told the believers in Colossae not to do
   and everything the legalists told them not to do. Make two
   separate lists, and if you mark up your Bible, use two different
   colors.

   _____

   _____

   _____

   _____

Interpretation

Verses 16-18: How often do we think about what other people are thinking about us? Some people in Paul's day were subjecting themselves to religious observances that had the appearance of spirituality but were actually external practices lacking depth. If our religious expression is for show, we'll be concerned with the audience's opinion. But if our religion is rooted in reverence for God, we'll be concerned only with His perspective. Many times, individuals become entangled in the superficial rituals of religion, which merely cast a "shadow" of genuine faith instead of representing the reality, which is Christ. Peer pressure can lead us to engage in meaningless spiritual rituals. As believers, our faith in Christ should be heartfelt, not a shallow checklist of dos and don'ts. The Colossian church was influenced by a kind of peer-pressure religiosity. They expressed their Christlikeness through external acts, which aren't the essence of faith. Paul directly tells the Colossians, "Do not let anyone judge you by what you eat or drink" (verse 16). In verse 18, Paul admonishes them, "Do not let anyone who delights in false humility and the worship of angels disqualify you."

I appreciate the insight from one commentator on this passage: "'His unspiritual mind puffs him up with idle notions,' which highlights the empty arrogance of the false teachers. . . . The 'mind of the flesh,' as it's literally termed in Greek, is the innate mindset devoid of the Holy Spirit's guidance. Such a mindset inflates the individual with unfounded pride, leading to a haughty attitude. These religious experiences might appear as genuine spiritual insights to the unenlightened mind. They might even become the benchmark for evaluating life's experiences, but they lack genuine authenticity and integrity."[5]

Verses 19-20: Paul is warning the church of Colossae that false teachers have lost contact with the head, Christ. They are trying to operate independently from the source, but ligaments cannot work or contribute to anything meaningful if the head is not working in tandem with the rest of the body. When I was in college, I sat wrong one day and somehow got a condition called drop foot. My foot would no longer flex. It was scary to look at my foot, try to move it, and only be able to drag it on the floor. It seems Paul is saying that some false teachers were like limping feet that weren't getting signals from the brain and were not working correctly.

Verses 22-23: In Colossians, Paul dedicates most of his writing to debunking perspectives that divert the Colossian church's attention from God to worldly matters. This ideology promoted the belief that deeds, rather than God, could redeem the Colossian church. According to Paul, if Christianity turns into mere performance or a set of rituals, then these actions "have, to be sure, the appearance of wisdom in self-made religion and self-abasement and severe treatment of the body, but are of no value against fleshly indulgence" (verse 23, NASB). This principle of not letting others judge or disqualify us for not adhering to "human commands and teachings" (verse 22) is deeply resonant with our human nature. Often, we allow others to influence us by overthinking their opinions about us. However, what God endorses isn't always popular among people.

Application

1. List out some of your own experiences with legalistic traditions. What impact have these traditions had on your faith?

   _____

   _____

   _____

   _____

2. In your own life, how can you urge others onward in growing an authentic faith of the heart rather than just following the rules?

   _____

   _____

   _____

   _____

3. This week, how can you engage with the substance of the gospel, not just a list of dos and don'ts?

_____

_____

_____

_____

Space for Reflection

_____

_____

_____

_____

_____

_____

_____

_____

_____

_____

_____

_____

_____

_____

_____

_____

_____

_____

Lord God,

I pray that I can stand firm against false teaching, that I would understand what the essence of the true gospel is. I pray that I may really be able to grasp through this Bible study the importance of Christ's work on my behalf.

Pray this personalized version of Colossians 2:2-3:

I pray that [I] may be encouraged in heart and united in love, so that [I] may have the full riches of complete understanding, in order that [I] may know the mystery of God, namely, Christ, in whom are hidden all the treasures of wisdom and knowledge.

Thank You, Lord, for all You do!

In Jesus' name, amen.

Final Thoughts

Video Notes

Week 3: Colossians 3

_____
_____
_____
_____
_____
_____
_____
_____
_____
_____
_____
_____
_____
_____
_____
_____
_____
_____
_____
_____

*Since, then, you have been raised with Christ, set your hearts on
things above, where Christ is, seated at the right hand of God. Set
your minds on things above, not on earthly things. For you died,
and your life is now hidden with Christ in God.*

COLOSSIANS 3:1-3

we give thanks to God, the Father of our Lord Jesus Christ. 4 For we have heard

Christ Jesus and your love for all of God's people, 5 which come from your confi

God has reserved for you in heaven. You have had this expectation ever since yo

he truth of the Good News. 6 This same Good News that came to you is going out al

t is bearing fruit everywhere by changing lives, just as it changed your lives fr

t heard and understood the truth about God's wonderful grace. 7 You learned ab

m Epaphras, our beloved co-worker. He is Christ's faithful servant, and he is h

behalf. 8 He has told us about the love for others that the Holy Spirit has given

not stopped praying for you since we first heard about you. We ask God to give yo

ge of his will and to give you spiritual wisdom and understanding. 10 Then the

l always honor and please the Lord, and your lives will produce every kind of g

while, you will grow as you learn to know God better and better. 11 We also pray

strengthened with all his glorious power so you will have all the endurance an

. May you be filled with joy, 12 always thanking the Father. He has enabled you

heritance that belongs to his people, who live in the light. 13 For he has rescu

dom of darkness and transferred us into the Kingdom of his dear Son, 14 who pur

and forgave our sins. 15 Christ is the visible image of the invisible God. He ex

was created and is supreme over all creation, 16 for through him God created e

avenly realms and on earth. He made the things we can see and the things we ca

hrones, kingdoms, rulers, and authorities in the unseen world. Everything was

him and for him. 17 He existed before anything else, and he holds all creation

also the head of the church, which is his body. He is the beginning, supreme o

the dead. So he is first in everything. 19 For God in all his fullness was plea

, 20 and through him God reconciled everything to himself. He made peace with

and on earth by means of Christ's blood on the cross. 21 This includes you who

from God. You were his enemies, separated from him by your evil thoughts and

w he has reconciled you to himself through the death of Christ in his physical

he has brought you into his own presence, and you are holy and blameless as y

m without a single fault. 23 But you must continue to believe this truth and st

't drift away from the assurance you received when you heard the Good News. T

been preached all over the world, and I, Paul, have been appointed as God's se

it. 24 I am glad when I suffer for you in my body, for I am participating in the

that continue for his body, the church. 25 God has given me the responsibility

h by proclaiming his entire message to you. 26 This message was kept secret fo

ations past, but now it has been revealed to God's people. 27 For God wanted th

WEEK 3

COLOSSIANS 3

WHEN I WAS A TEENAGER LIVING IN THAILAND, I got my name tattooed on my hip in Thai. Yes, a sure moment of rebellion, and now I live with the fact that my name is permanently inked on my body in a different language. I find it more than humorous that, as a sixteen-year-old, I thought this was a great idea. More recently, my husband surprised me with a new license plate that had my name on it: MIK3LLA with a *3* in place of the *E*. When I drive around town, everyone—and I mean *everyone*—knows who is in the driver's seat.

Colossians 3 is about living up to our name—our new name. As Christ followers, we bear the name of Christ and show others how He works through how we live our lives. Instead of trying to live up to our earthly name, we need to live up to what Paul says in this chapter of Colossians: "Since, then, you have been raised with Christ, set your hearts on things above, where Christ is, seated at the right hand of God. Set your minds on things above, not on earthly things" (verses 1-2).

But we don't do this through our own effort, righteousness, or hard work. We can only do it by the power of the Holy Spirit and His work on our behalf. We die with Christ, then rise with Him in new life. Setting our hearts and minds on things above means we are committed to not putting worldly things before our eyes. As Psalm 101:3 says, "I will not look with approval on anything that is vile."

Our Christian conduct changes how we act and what we do by the power of the Spirit. Our fleshly nature is dead. Paul shows us what characterizes a Christian. Christians live in peace, and they are compassionate and kind. They look different from the world because they continue to put to death their earthly nature. Every day we get to choose whether to live with integrity. It becomes not about our will, but His will. We conform to the image of Christ by choosing Him day in and day out. I love how Spurgeon puts it:

> The Christian, while in the world, is not to be of the world. He should be distinguished from it in the great object of his life. To him, "to live" should be "Christ." Whether he eats or drinks or whatever he does, he should do it all to God's glory. You may lay up treasure; but lay it up in heaven, where neither moth nor rust destroy, where thieves do not break in and steal. You may work to be rich; but make it your ambition to be "rich in faith" and good works. You may pursue pleasure; but when you are happy, sing psalms and make melody in your hearts to the Lord. In your spirit, as well as in your aim, you should differ from the world. Waiting humbly before God, always conscious of His presence, delighting in fellowship with Him, and seeking to know His will, you will prove that you are a citizen of heaven.[1]

When we desire more of Christ, we find ourselves craving more of what He wants. Our desires change over time to mirror His. But this happens out of an overflow of our new life in Christ. When we put our faith in Christ, we become new creatures, and with that our desires change.

As we grow, we see our specific desires conform to Christ's. We might find that certain things we used to yearn for have lost their hold on us, and new yearnings have sprung up. Paul was a man of great passion and zeal, and we see that he wanted his own desires to conform to Christ's.

e strengthened with all his glorious power so you will have all the endurance
ed. May you be filled with joy, 12 always thanking the Father. He has enabled
inheritance that belongs to his people, who live in the light. 13 For he has re
ngdom of darkness and transferred us into the Kingdom of his dear Son, 14 who
m and forgave our sins. 15 Christ is the visible image of the invisible God. He
ing was created and is supreme over all creation. 16 for through him God create
heavenly realms and on ... e can see and the things w
s thrones, kingdoms, rul ... nseen world. Everything
h him and for him. 17 He ... se, and he holds all creati
is also the head of the ... e is the beginning, suprem
om the dead. So he is first in everything. 19 For God in all his fullness was p
1st, 20 and through him God reconciled everything to himself. He made peace w
ven and on earth by means of Christ's blood on the cross. 21 This includes you

Day One
Read all of Colossians 3.

Focus Verses

Colossians 3:1-4

Observation

1. Look up the word *set* in a dictionary, and write down the
   definition.

   _____

   _____

   _____

2. Read Philippians 4:8, and write down the things Paul says we
   should think about. What similarities do you notice between this
   passage and Colossians 3:1-4?

   _____

   _____

   _____

   _____

Interpretation

Verse 1: Paul is essentially saying we should align our hearts' desires with Christ's. We should humbly look up and let our hearts and minds be subject to His lordship. What we give our attention will end up forming us. Where we focus our energy is who we will become. This verse reminds us that we all have been raised with Christ, which means we identify with His death and resurrection, and we are spiritually made new. We are born again, or regenerated from death to life. He is both our ruler and the One who controls the cosmos. He is awaiting the time that He will prop His feet on His enemies, making them His footstool (see Hebrews 10:12-13). Aligning ourselves with the reality of His authority, trusting His leadership enough that our hearts' desires are set on Him, and reminding ourselves of His rightful place in our lives will keep us from panicking about the future and bring peace to our hearts and minds.

Verse 2-3: One implication of a life rooted in Christ is that we choose to think about "things above"—we maintain a heavenly perspective. When we are assailed by hardship and temptation, we pause and see it through the lens of God's Word. Paul says that we have died and are hidden in Christ. This means that Christ took the punishment for our sins, and now He is our covering. We hide not from Him but *in* Him, knowing that His righteousness is imputed to us, or viewed by God as if it is our righteousness too. According to the *Life Application Study Bible*, to be hidden in Christ means to be "concealed and safe."[2] When we are hidden in Christ, we live in light of what is true. We put away sinful desires, resist temptation, and walk in the Spirit because He has made us new.

Verse 4: Often, we see ourselves and our identities in many ways, but we do not see Christ as "[our] life." William Barclay explains this concept so well: "This is the kind of peak of devotion which we can only dimly understand and only haltingly and imperfectly express. Sometimes we say of a man, 'Music is his life. Sport is his life. He lives for his work.' Such a man finds life and all that it means in music, in sport, in work, as the case may be. For the Christian, Christ is his life."[3] This verse also shows us that we have been raised with Christ in glory! As Ephesians 2:6 says, "God raised us up with Christ and seated us with him in the heavenly realms in Christ Jesus." Whenever I face conflict in a personal relationship with a brother or sister in Christ, I think about how they, too, are seated with Christ. I picture them right next to Jesus, seated at His right hand.

Application

1. What are some differences between the heart and the mind? Give one practical example of setting your heart on things above and one of setting your mind on things above.

_____

_____

_____

_____

2. How can you fight the temptations of the flesh and instead walk in the newness of life in Christ? How might the truth that your life is hidden in Christ help you do this?

_____

_____

_____

_____

Space for Reflection

_____
_____
_____
_____
_____
_____
_____
_____
_____
_____
_____
_____
_____
_____
_____
_____
_____
_____
_____
_____
_____
_____
_____
_____
_____
_____

be strengthened with all his glorious power so you will have all the endurance
need. May you be filled with joy, 12 always thanking the Father. He has enabled
e inheritance that belongs to his people, who live in the light. 13 For he has re
ingdom of darkness and transferred us into the Kingdom of his dear Son, 14 who
om and forgave our sins. 15 Christ is the visible image of the invisible God. He
ing was created and is supreme over all creation. 16 for through him God create
e heavenly realms and on   e can see and the things w
as thrones, kingdoms, rul   unseen world. Everything
gh him and for him. 17 He   se, and he holds all creati
t is also the head of the   e is the beginning, suprem
rom the dead. So he is first in everything. 19 For God in all his fullness was p
rist, 20 and through him God reconciled everything to himself. He made peace w
aven and on earth by means of Christ's blood on the cross. 21 This includes you

Day Two

Focus Verses

Colossians 3:5-10

Observation

1. Highlight or list any imperatives (commands) in this passage.

   To read more about observing a Bible passage by making lists,
   turn to page 128 of Chasing Sacred.

   _____

   _____

   _____

2. Think about the context. What grace-driven truths listed right
   before this passage enable us to follow its instructions?

   _____

   _____

   _____

   _____

Interpretation

Verses 5-9: By God's grace, we can now put off our old sinful ways. "Put to death" is a strong instruction to kill that which is sinful in us. When we understand that we are seated at the right hand of the Father, it motivates us to live differently. When I go to a fine-dining restaurant, I dress differently, act differently, and eat differently than I would at a fast-food place. Similarly, knowing that I am seated next to Christ, I need to straighten my posture because my position is prominent. When we understand our position in Christ, we become distinct from the rest of the world. In this passage, there are two lists of sins, some more grievous in nature and others that seem less significant. As David Guzik says, "The sins Paul next lists (anger, wrath, and so forth) are regarded by many as 'little' sins that Christians may overlook with little danger. Paul challenges us to put off the old man in *every* area of our lives."[4]

We must not make allowance for any of these sins—big or small. All of them are sins against God, and we should seek to put them off and to walk in the ways of Christ. We cannot put off these sins on our own; we must walk in the power of the Spirit within us as we strive to honor God in every way.

Verse 10: In our new lives as Christ followers, we must be conformed to Him. In every word and deed, we should point others to Christ. We do this by putting on our new self. Christ is now our ultimate example. I have a friend who is like a generator: she converts passion for Christ into energetic living for Him. Her inner life overflows into her outer life: what she reads in the Word propels her toward living it out. May what we put on and practice match what we profess. May those who leave a conversation with us be encouraged to move forward in their desire for Christ.

Application

1. In these lists of sins, which ones do you struggle with the most? What are some ways you can put off these sins?

   _____

   _____

   _____

2. How are you actively using your day to renew your knowledge of the Creator? Scripture memory? Bible study? Prayer? How can you more effectively integrate these habits into your day?

   _____

   _____

   _____

Space for Reflection

_____

_____

_____

_____

_____

_____

_____

_____

_____

_____

_____

Day Three

Focus Verses

Colossians 3:11-14

Observation

1. Look up the definitions of three of the virtues listed in verse 12.
   Did any of these definitions surprise you?

   _____

   _____

   _____

2. Paraphrase this passage in one to two sentences.

   _____

   _____

   _____

   _____

   _____

Interpretation

Verse 11: There are no longer racial barriers or distinctions that separate Christ followers from the love that binds us together. Our union with Christ makes it possible for us to unite with one another. We are no longer categorized by our earthly class but are given a heavenly status.

Verse 12: Clothing is visible; it is an exterior expression of an inward reality. Clothing ourselves with compassion, kindness, humility, gentleness, and patience means those traits are evident to those around us. We are chosen, holy, and dearly loved. Therefore, we should love others.

Verse 13: The word translated "bear with" can also be translated as "endure, have patience with, suffer, admit, persist."[5] We must bear with others and be willing to forgive when we have a grievance against them. It is easy to hold on to bitterness or to grow in resentment. What is not easy is to forgive. I pray over my son Barkley three things every night: that he would abound in love, be slow to anger, and be quick to forgive. For it is easy in my human condition to feel a lack of love, be quick to anger, and often be very slow to forgive. But that is the opposite of what characterizes believers in Christ, who remember that the Lord first forgave us.

Verse 14: Love is the crown of the virtues. It binds them all together. Looking at the divides in our country, it's clear that most people speak out of pride in their own knowledge rather than love. Back in New Testament times, the Colossian church struggled with this issue as well. Throughout Colossians 2, Paul addressed the Colossians about their pride coming from their "spiritual" wisdom. When judgment comes, God will not ask whether we were *right*. Instead He will ask, How did we love?

Application

1. How does Paul describe God's chosen people in this passage? How might it affect your daily life if you remembered you are holy and dearly loved?

_____

_____

_____

2. Write down any parts of the passage that have to do with how the gospel affects your relationships with other people. How could you apply these to your relationships this week?

_____

_____

_____

Space for Reflection

_____

_____

_____

_____

_____

_____

_____

_____

_____

_____

Focus Verses

Colossians 3:15-17

Observation

1. Highlight or list every mention of thanksgiving or gratitude in this passage.

   _____

   _____

   _____

2. List the three ways that the message of Christ is supposed to dwell in us.

   _____

   _____

   _____

   _____

   _____

Interpretation

Verse 15: Peace and gratitude should characterize every Christian. Our hearts should be ruled by peace, not divisiveness. In a society where anxiety is at an all-time high, how distinct would we be if peace governed our decisions? In all of Paul's salutations, he prays for the believers' peace. Peace is a bond that brings all believers together, and thankfulness is the resounding song of a believer who understands the degree of pardon and grace in their life.

The word *rule* here means "umpire."[6] When we read, "Let the peace of Christ rule in your hearts," we can envision an umpire keeping our hearts out of sinful, disordered living that characterized our old lives before we knew Christ. I like to use a baseball analogy to teach my children about their emotions.

I tell them, "Life is going to throw many balls at you! You may discover a good friend betrayed you or talked badly about you. Your brother might take a toy from you. All of a sudden, a surprise ball like that comes flying out of nowhere, and you catch it. You have to look at the ball and explain your emotion out loud: 'I feel angry!'

"Now you must decide how to respond. Will the peace of Christ be your umpire? Will you handle the situation in a constructive way, such as discussing the matter or seeking reconciliation? Or will you react in a way that disrupts the game? The umpire is the one who makes all the calls."

When the world throws a ball at you, how are you going to act? Many will blame the umpire when their world is in upheaval, and many will blame Jesus for the bad things that happen in their lives. But the truth is that the umpire—the peace that can only come from God—should govern our reactions when it's game time.

Verse 16: When the message of Christ dwells in you richly, you are able to encourage those around you. You are so full of wisdom that it bursts out of you, and the song encourages your fellow workers in Christ.

If the Word of God has found a home in you, it should spill forth to richly and generously bless others. This verse really convicts me to memorize Scripture so the Word of God can find its home in me! When my dad came out of surgery after getting his kidney removed, he was on a lot of medication. He was so loopy, but what came spilling out? Verses came tumbling out of his mouth even when he was not coherent. I pray that verses will pour out of me like that one day!

Verse 17: Do everything in the name of the Lord, and give thanks for everything. Our reputations show others what He is like. Are we representing His name well? We bear His name in the grocery store line, in the comment sections of social media, and in the secret spaces of our homes.

Application

1. **Grateful Christians are hard to come by.** Why do you think Paul constantly wrote about being thankful (for example, in Colossians 3:17)? What is one practical way you can add more thanksgiving to your life?

2. How are singing and worshiping connected to gratefulness?

3. **Sin breeds in isolation.** Are there any areas of your life that you feel do not represent God's name?

Space for Reflection

Day Five

Focus Verses

Colossians 3:18-25

Observation

1. Highlight or list all the relationships mentioned in this passage, along with the instructions given for each.

   _____

   _____

   _____

2. What does it mean to "submit . . . as is fitting in the Lord" (verse 18)? (Hint: read verses 22-23 again.)

   _____

   _____

   _____

   _____

   _____

3. Read the interpretation section below and write down what a Greco-Roman household was like during this time period. What did slavery look like in the Greco-Roman world?

_____

_____

_____

Interpretation

Verse 18: Here we see some household codes that are characteristic of the first-century Greco-Roman households. Paul establishes that all submission should be exercised under the Lord, "as is fitting in the Lord." Furthermore, this nuanced term for submission can mean various things depending on the context of the passage and what voice it is said in. Let's consult a commentary to understand what it means in this verse. "The term does not suggest slavery or servitude, and certainly never calls for the husband to make his wife submit. If he could, her heart would not be in it. Besides, Paul addressed wives here, not husbands. In this context, the word differs radically from the word which describes the role of children and slaves who are to obey."[7]

Verse 19: Husbands are called to love, care, and show kindness to their wives. This is called agape love. This type of love takes great sacrifice. Husbands must display self-forgetfulness. They need to deal gently with their wives.

Verses 20-21: Paul urges children to obey and listen to their parents. He also asks fathers not to irritate or discourage their children. We must learn to encourage our children to crush their sin without crushing their spirit with constant nagging or passive-aggressive discipline.

Verse 22: Paul calls on slaves to obey and show the fruits of their walk with the Lord even under difficult circumstances. These passages can be confusing as we know that all people are created in God's image. We may wonder why Paul didn't call for the end of the institution of slavery. One commentary responds to the question like this: "It seems that Paul should have written to undermine the institution of slavery or at least to encourage the revolt of the slaves. On the one hand, to do so, would have caused significant difficulty in the first-century setting, and undue persecution would result. Besides, Christians could do little by force. On the other hand, the teaching of the apostle here and elsewhere clearly sowed the seed for the emancipation of slaves and the end of the institution. Paul did what he could in the best way possible."[8]

Verses 23-24: These verses promise a reward for working for the Lord and stewarding our relationships in our homes well. Serving and giving of ourselves in relationships can be very difficult, but we are called to do all things out of our reverence and love for the Lord.

Verse 25: Paul tells us that there should be no favoritism in any relationship. He turns our eyes to treating people justly in all relationships. Throughout today's passage, Paul is concerned about order within human relationships. Our relationships have the potential to show others that God's Kingdom is orderly, not chaotic. Many would claim relationship dynamics vary by culture and time period, but here we see that these directives are universal. Our relationships function the way they should when we submit to each other out of reverence and love. Relationships are patterned after the Trinity, so servanthood should characterize them.

Application

1. **It is easy to get caught up in people-pleasing or applause.** How can you follow Paul's guidance in verse 23: "Whatever you do, work at it with all your heart, as working for the Lord, not for human masters"?

2. Think about your own relationships. What can you apply to them from this passage of Scripture? Read Ephesians 5:22–6:9 as well to gain even more insight on this subject.

_____

_____

_____

_____

Lord God,

Thank You that my old life has died and now I have a new life in Christ. Guide me to focus on things that are honorable and worthy. I pray that my character would reflect the reality that my life is now hidden in You. Help me to grow in compassion, kindness, humility, gentleness, and patience. Help my life be ruled by the peace that only You can give. Thank You for all the joy I receive because I know You.

In Jesus' name, amen.

Final Thoughts

Video Notes

Week 4: Colossians 4

---

*Devote yourselves to prayer, being watchful and thankful. And pray
for us, too, that God may open a door for our message, so that we may
proclaim the mystery of Christ, for which I am in chains. Pray that I
may proclaim it clearly, as I should. Be wise in the way you act toward
outsiders; make the most of every opportunity. Let your conversation
be always full of grace, seasoned with salt, so that you may know
how to answer everyone.*

COLOSSIANS 4:2-6

we give thanks to God, the Father of our Lord Jesus Christ. 4 For we have heard
Christ Jesus and your love for all of God's people, 5 which come from your confi
God has reserved for you in heaven. You have had this expectation ever since yo
he truth of the Good News. 6 This same Good News that came to you is going out a
t is bearing fruit everywhere by changing lives, just as it changed your lives f
t heard and understood the truth about God's wonderful grace. 7 You learned ab
om Epaphras, our beloved co-worker. He is Christ's faithful servant, and he is h
behalf. 8 He has told us about the love for others that the Holy Spirit has give
not stopped praying for you since we first heard about you. We ask God to give y
ge of his will and to give you spiritual wisdom and understanding. 10 Then the
l always honor and please the Lord, and your lives will produce every kind of g
while, you will grow as you learn to know God better and better. 11 We also pray
strengthened with all his glorious power so you will have all the endurance a
. May you be filled with joy, 12 always thanking the Father. He has enabled you
nheritance that belongs to his people, who live in the light. 13 For he has rescu
rdom of darkness and transferred us into the Kingdom of his dear Son, 14 who pu
and forgave our sins. 15 Christ is the visible image of the invisible God. He ex
g was created and is supreme over all creation, 16 for through him God created
eavenly realms and on earth. He made the things we can see and the things we c
thrones, kingdoms, rulers, and authorities in the unseen world. Everything wa
him and for him. 17 He existed before anything else, and he holds all creation
s also the head of the church, which is his body. He is the beginning, supreme
m the dead. So he is first in everything. 19 For God in all his fullness was ple
t, 20 and through him God reconciled everything to himself. He made peace wit
en and on earth by means of Christ's blood on the cross. 21 This includes you wh
from God. You were his enemies, separated from him by your evil thoughts and
ow he has reconciled you to himself through the death of Christ in his physica
, he has brought you into his own presence, and you are holy and blameless as
im without a single fault. 23 But you must continue to believe this truth and
n't drift away from the assurance you received when you heard the Good News.
s been preached all over the world, and I, Paul, have been appointed as God's s
m it. 24 I am glad when I suffer for you in my body, for I am participating in the
t that continue for his body, the church. 25 God has given me the responsibilit
rch by proclaiming his entire message to you. 26 This message was kept secret
erations past, but now it has been revealed to God's people. 27 For God wanted t

be strengthened with all his glorious power so you will have all the endurance
eed. May you be filled with joy, 12 always thanking the Father. He has enabled
e inheritance that belongs to his people, who live in the light. 13 For he has re
ingdom of darkness and transferred us into the Kingdom of his dear Son, 14 who
om and forgave our sins. 15 Christ is the visible image of the invisible God. He
ning was created and is supreme over all creation, 16 for through him God create
e heavenly realms a   see and the things w
as thrones, kingdoms   world. Everything
gh him and for him.   d he holds all creati
t is also the head of   he beginning, suprem
rom the dead. So he is first in everything. 19 For God in all his fullness was p
rist, 20 and through him God reconciled everything to himself. He made peace w
aven and on earth by means of Christ's blood on the cross. 21 This includes you

WEEK 4

COLOSSIANS 4

ONCE, WHEN WE WERE ON VACATION, my son stumbled upon a secret doorway. We were exploring our Airbnb, an apartment overlooking the gorgeous ocean. We walked down the stairs, and a full-length mirror caught my eye. As I peered into the glass, I checked out my hair, noted the weight I still needed to lose post-baby, and thought about the day's plans. My five-year-old quickly caught up with me and curiously grabbed the side of the mirror. All of a sudden, it swung open to reveal a hidden doorway. I was stunned that I had been so busy thinking about myself when behind this mirror was a doorway to a surprise storage facility in which lay everything needed for the building to be maintained. Often we are so busy anxiously thinking about today's details or trying to keep up with all the tasks that are before us that we forget that behind the smallest details of our day is a God who cares—and prayers that need to be prayed. It is so easy for us to get wrapped up in ourselves, our world, and the frustrations of our day.

One study from 2020 said that every day we process around six thousand thoughts, and another quick Google search said that 80 percent of our thoughts are negative.[1] But I wonder how many of our thoughts are focused on ourselves. One of my favorite quotes is from Dallas Willard, who says, "The first and most basic thing we can and must do is to keep

God before our minds."[2] David learned this and wrote, "I have set the LORD continually before me; because He is at my right hand, I will not be shaken. Therefore my heart is glad and my glory rejoices; my flesh also will dwell securely" (Psalm 16:8-9, NASB). We must fight to think of God always at the forefront of our minds whether we're waiting in the school pickup line, doing dishes, or sitting in our office chair. Fighting to spend our days being prayerfully committed to those around us means we must notice their needs.

Our prayers often follow the trajectory of our thoughts. How often are we thinking of those around us? In Colossians 4, Paul reminds us how committed he was to praying for the saints, as well as how many ministry partners he had. It is painful at times to set aside our own agenda to serve another. Self-forgetfulness is the rarest form of Christian virtue. It is easy to live our lives staring into a mirror without thought of our Christian brother and sister or praying on their behalf. Paul opens the door in this chapter for us to see what it looks like to spend our days interceding on behalf of others.

Focus Verses

Colossians 4:1-4

Observation

1. Highlight or list what Paul tells the Colossians to devote
   themselves to.

   _____

   _____

   _____

   _____

2. What does Paul ask them to pray for?

   _____

   _____

   _____

   _____

Interpretation

Verse 1: This verse is part of Paul's instruction to the church about how they should look to an unbelieving world. He exhorted masters to be fair to their slaves. (For more on this subject, read the section "A Note on Slavery" on page 100 of this study.) Today, employers can take this verse to heart by treating their employees with respect, remembering that God is watching. As God oversees us, we have the responsibility to oversee others in service and dedication. This means patiently bearing with those who can be frustrating to employ.

Verse 2: We often spend so much time in prayer asking God to change our circumstances, yet we spend so little time waiting patiently and watching with intention for those prayers to be answered. Once they *are* answered, it's easy to forget to thank God and quickly move on to the next request. I have prayed many prayers for my marriage over the years. Once God answered them, I forgot to thank Him for the answer with the same amount of fervor I prayed with.

I love this Spurgeon quote: "Prayer should be mingled with praise. I have heard that in New England after the Puritans had settled there a long while, they used to have very often a day of humiliation, fasting, and prayer, till they had so many days of fasting, humiliation, and prayer, that at last a good senator proposed that they should change it for once, and have a day of thanksgiving."[3] No wonder Paul continually reminds us to thank God! Let's set aside time in our prayer life to thank God for what He has done.

Verses 3-4: Paul asks the church to pray for him to speak the gospel clearly and to make known the mystery of Christ—salvation. He was in prison when he wrote these words, which makes his diligent faith and desire to share the gospel even more amazing. He wrote letters from prison to encourage the churches far and wide, and these letters encourage us today. Scholars say Paul wrote Ephesians, Philippians, and Philemon around the same time as writing Colossians.

Like Paul, we can also ask God to provide opportunities in our daily lives to preach the gospel. We often overcomplicate it. We do not need platforms or stages to do this. We can intentionally pray that God would show us the people He wants us to talk to, encourage, or witness to. Watch as He shows you who those people are!

Application

1. Ask the Lord for an opportunity to share the gospel with a neighbor, grocery store clerk, family member, or other person in your everyday life this week. Begin each day by praying intentionally that God would bring someone for you to encourage, witness to, or shine the light of Christ to by your love.

2. Read Luke 17:11-19 and meditate on both being the one leper who returned to thank Jesus—and also being one of the nine who did not return. How does this help you see the need for gratitude in your own life?

Space for Reflection

strengthened with all his glorious power so you will have all the endurance a
d. May you be filled with joy, 12 always thanking the Father. He has enabled you
nheritance that belongs to his people, who live in the light. 13 For he has rescu
rdom of darkness and transferred us into the Kingdom of his dear Son, 14 who pu
a and forgave our sins. 15 Christ is the visible image of the invisible God. He ex
g was created and is supreme over all creation. 16 for through him God created
eavenly realms and on ear   n see and the things we c
thrones, kingdoms, rulers,   een world. Everything wa
a him and for him. 17 He ex   and he holds all creation
s also the head of the chu   s the beginning, supreme o
m the dead. So he is first in everything. 19 For God in all his fullness was ple
st, 20 and through him God reconciled everything to himself. He made peace wit
an and on earth by means of Christ's blood on the cross. 21 This includes you wh

Focus Verses

Colossians 4:5-6

Observation

1. How does Paul direct the Colossians to act toward outsiders?

   _____

   _____

   _____

   _____

2. Highlight or list the two things that should characterize a
   believer's speech.

   _____

   _____

   _____

   _____

Interpretation

Verses 5-6: Paul admonishes the Colossians on how they should live. As one scholar says, "It remains true that the reputation of the gospel is bound up with the behavior of those who claim to have experienced its saving power. People who do not read the Bible for themselves or listen to the preaching of the Word of God can see the lives of those who do, and can form their judgment accordingly. Let Christians make full use, then, of the present season of opportunity."[4]

We must consider how we interact with unbelievers and how we behave when we're around them. Every interaction—whether with a taxi driver, flight attendant, family member, employee, or Instacart delivery person—is an opportunity for us to display the gospel in action. People should find that when we talk, our words are seasoned with salt—or as the New Living Translation says it, "gracious and attractive"—and make them want more interaction. They should be touched by our kindness, positivity, and encouragement. "Full of grace" means we are unoffended, understanding, and kind, no matter the disposition of the person we're talking to. Do they need prayer? Do they need encouragement? We should be so sensitive to the needs of those around us. This is only possible by the power of the Holy Spirit working in us and strengthening us.

Application

1. Pray that the Spirit would help you answer someone carefully this week, taking into consideration what they might need to hear for gospel encouragement. Did you notice any opportunities arise in answer to your prayer?

---

2. List a few people who do not know the gospel that you can be praying for.

_____

_____

_____

_____

Space for Reflection

_____

_____

_____

_____

_____

_____

_____

_____

_____

_____

_____

_____

_____

_____

_____

_____

_____

Day Three

be strengthened with all his glorious power so you will have all the enduranc...
...eed. May you be filled with joy, 12 always thanking the Father. He has enabled...
...e inheritance that belongs to his people, who live in the light. 13 For he has re...
...kingdom of darkness and transferred us into the Kingdom of his dear Son, 14 who...
...dom and forgave our sins. 15 Christ is the visible image of the invisible God. He...
...hing was created and is supreme over all creation. 16 for through him God creat...
...e heavenly realms and o... ...can see and the things w...
...as thrones, kingdoms, ru... ...nseen world. Everything...
...ugh him and for him. 17 H... ...e, and he holds all creat...
...st is also the head of the... ...is the beginning, suprem...
...from the dead. So he is first in everything. 19 For God in all his fullness was...
...rist, 20 and through him God reconciled everything to himself. He made peace...
...aven and on earth by means of Christ's blood on the cross. 21 This includes you...

Focus Verses

Colossians 4:7-9

Observation

1. Who were Tychicus and Onesimus? For information about these men, consult a trusted commentary (see appendix C for recommendations) or check the notes in your study Bible.

   _____

   _____

   _____

2. How does Paul describe each of these fellow ministers in the gospel?

   _____

   _____

   _____

   _____

Interpretation

Verses 7-8: Tychicus was the messenger who carried this letter from Paul. Paul writes, "I am sending him to you for the express purpose that you may know about our circumstances and that he may encourage your hearts" (verse 8). When someone sent a letter in the ancient world, it had to be someone who was trustworthy. Usually there was a specific occasion for which the letter was being sent, and we know that for the church at Colossae, part of the occasion was the false teaching spreading through the church body.

Verse 9: Onesimus was a slave who escaped his master and met Paul in Rome. There, Onesimus became a believer, and Paul wrote a letter about him: the book of Philemon. You can read more about his situation in week 5 of this Bible study.

Application

1. Reach out to two prayer partners or confidantes—people you share life with and whom you count on spiritually—and send them a word of encouragement today.

2. Pray for those same two spiritual confidantes, that they will be found faithful and will be able to encourage the hearts of those around them.

Space for Reflection

Day Four

Focus Verses

Colossians 4:10-15

Observation

1. Highlight or list everyone who is mentioned in this passage and how Paul describes them.

   _____

   _____

   _____

   _____

2. Do more research on one or two of the people mentioned in these passages. Fine-tune your research skills by using some of the trusted commentaries in appendix C, or even downloading a free version of Logos Bible Software (logos.com/free-edition) to help.

Interpretation

Verses 10-15: This passage lists several different friends of Paul who came alongside him in ministry. Aristarchus traveled with Paul. One commentary says, "When Paul took up the collection for the Jewish saints, Aristarchus was selected to accompany the money to Jerusalem (Acts 20:4). He remained with Paul on the journey to Rome (Acts 27:2). In Colossians 4:10, Paul called him a 'fellow prisoner,' presumably in prison for the same reasons as Paul, and he was one of three Jewish believers who were with Paul at the time (4:11)."[5]

John Mark is mentioned in different places as a companion of Paul (see Acts 13:5). We know he was on Paul's first missionary journey alongside Barnabas and then left for some time, which caused division between Paul and Barnabas. Luke played a significant role in the early church, and he seems to have been with Paul through many of his travels (see Colossians 4:14, 2 Timothy 4:11, and Philemon 24:2).

Reading the names of all these ministry partners shows how purposeful God is in selecting and helping us find the people we need to come alongside us. I have often been encouraged by someone texting me, praying for me, or supporting me in the midst of a difficult season in ministry. I see God's purposeful hand in the friendships and partners He has given me to spread the gospel. Luke stayed with Paul throughout much of his ministry journey, but that's not always how ministry works. We are not always the ones who work together with another individual teacher or preacher. Sometimes we have roles of leadership. Other times we have more behind-the-scenes responsibilities as partners in prayer and encouragement. Whatever season we're in, we can partner with others in ministry.

Application

1. Do you have any partners who help you encourage and connect with people in everyday life? If not, pray for God to show you people you can partner with in ministry.

2. **Paul vouched for Epaphras: "He is working hard for you and for those at Laodicea and Hierapolis" (verse 13).** When has someone vouched for you in your own life, and how can you vouch for others in your sphere of influence?

Space for Reflection

strengthened with all his glorious power so you will have all the endurance an
d. May you be filled with joy, 12 always thanking the Father. He has enabled you
nheritance that belongs to his people, who live in the light. 13 For he has rescu
dom of darkness and transferred us into the Kingdom of his dear Son, 14 who pu
and forgave our sins. 15 Christ is the visible image of the invisible God. He ex
g was created and is supreme over all creation. 16 for through him God created
eavenly realms and on ear   n see and the things we c
thrones, kingdoms, rulers,   en world. Everything wa
him and for him. 17 He ex   and he holds all creation
s also the head of the chu   the beginning, supreme o
m the dead. So he is first in everything. 19 For God in all his fullness was ple
st, 20 and through him God reconciled everything to himself. He made peace wit
en and on earth by means of Christ's blood on the cross. 21 This includes you wh

Focus Verses

Colossians 4:16-18

Observation

1. Why do you think Paul asked that this letter be read aloud to the
   Laodiceans?

   _____

   _____

   _____

   _____

2. How does Paul end his letter to the Colossians (verse 18)?

   _____

   _____

   _____

   _____

Interpretation

Verses 16-17: Paul ends this letter with a few instructions. He tells Archippus to "complete the ministry you have received in the Lord" (verse 17). It is easy to begin a new venture, but to complete something is an entirely different matter. When false teaching jeopardizes our endeavors or hardship threatens to disrupt what we have worked so hard to protect, it is especially challenging. If you have ever been in ministry, sometimes it can feel like one hardship after another. It is easy to want to give up when everything feels incredibly taxing and exhausting. Paul is urging the church to keep going and to endure with patience. He would not need to encourage Archippus to "complete the ministry" if ministry were always easy.

Verse 18: Paul leaves us with the statement "Remember my chains." Paul's life serves as a visible reminder that no matter our circumstances, the gospel can still advance. When we experience hardship, God can work through that hardship to further His Kingdom. Like Paul, we can face great opposition in ministry, but God is still in control. A commitment to Christ does not mean a life of ease, and doing good for the gospel does not always mean a thriving, bustling ministry. Sometimes God speaks through our sorrows and disappointments and allows us to go through very difficult situations where we feel chained to our circumstances.

Application

1. Reflect on someone you can encourage or spur on the way Paul does for Archippus in this passage. List a few individuals right now.

2. Think about a time that God called you to endure with patience in ministry. How did He encourage you in the midst of the hardship?

_____

_____

_____

_____

_____

Lord God,

Thank You for all the people You have brought alongside me in life who have encouraged me and brought me comfort in hard times.

Help me to make the most of every opportunity. Help me to see the ways You are strengthening me in ministry and bringing community alongside me that is encouraging and uplifting. Give me the desire to be more devoted to prayer and thanksgiving. Thank You for all the truths that You have outlined in Your Word!

In Jesus' name, amen.

Final Thoughts

Video Notes

Week 5: Philemon

_____

_____

_____

_____

_____

_____

_____

_____

_____

_____

_____

_____

_____

_____

_____

_____

_____

_____

*Perhaps the reason he was separated from you for a little while
was that you might have him back forever—no longer as a slave,
but better than a slave, as a dear brother.*

PHILEMON 1:15-16

we give thanks to God, the Father of our Lord Jesus Christ. 4 For we have heard
Christ Jesus and your love for all of God's people, 5 which come from your conf
God has reserved for you in heaven. You have had this expectation ever since yo
the truth of the Good News. 6 This same Good News that came to you is going out a
t is bearing fruit everywhere by changing lives, just as it changed your lives f
t heard and understood the truth about God's wonderful grace. 7 You learned ab
om Epaphras, our beloved co-worker. He is Christ's faithful servant, and he is h
behalf. 8 He has told us about the love for others that the Holy Spirit has give
not stopped praying for you since we first heard about you. We ask God to give
ge of his will and to give you spiritual wisdom and understanding. 10 Then the
l always honor and please the Lord, and your lives will produce every kind of g
while, you will grow as you learn to know God better and better. 11 We also pray
strengthened with all his glorious power so you will have all the endurance a
d. May you be filled with joy, 12 always thanking the Father. He has enabled you
nheritance that belongs to his people, who live in the light. 13 For he has resc
rdom of darkness and transferred us into the Kingdom of his dear Son, 14 who pu
and forgave our sins. 15 Christ is the visible image of the invisible God. He ex
g was created and is supreme over all creation, 16 for through him God created
eavenly realms and on earth. He made the things we can see and the things we
thrones, kingdoms, rulers, and authorities in the unseen world. Everything wa
him and for him. 17 He existed before anything else, and he holds all creation
s also the head of the church, which is his body. He is the beginning, supreme
m the dead. So he is first in everything. 19 For God in all his fullness was ple
t, 20 and through him God reconciled everything to himself. He made peace wit
en and on earth by means of Christ's blood on the cross. 21 This includes you wh
from God. You were his enemies, separated from him by your evil thoughts and
ow he has reconciled you to himself through the death of Christ in his physica
, he has brought you into his own presence, and you are holy and blameless as
im without a single fault. 23 But you must continue to believe this truth and
n't drift away from the assurance you received when you heard the Good News.
s been preached all over the world, and I, Paul, have been appointed as God's se
m it. 24 I am glad when I suffer for you in my body, for I am participating in the
st that continue for his body, the church. 25 God has given me the responsibilit
rch by proclaiming his entire message to you. 26 This message was kept secret
erations past, but now it has been revealed to God's people. 27 For God wanted

EARLY ON IN MY MARRIAGE, there was a period of time when my relationship with my husband was based on merit, not grace! To be honest, I was nursing a grudge that resulted in bitterness and resentment toward him for something that happened early on in our marriage. If you were a fly on the wall, you might notice that I took offense in almost every interaction. Bitterness and resentment had become the invisible third wheel in our relationship. I didn't enjoy it, but I also didn't know how to change it. I'd think, *And why should I have to be the one to change it? I wasn't the one in the wrong!* So instead of forgiving my husband, my lens was always focused on how he'd hurt me, and this produced a love that was calculated and certainly not overflowing or full of grace. I felt that he had an unpaid debt, of which I often reminded him. My love was based on what I felt he deserved. It was only by God's kindness that He spoke deeply into my own heart about His grace toward me, which amazingly delivered me to extend overflowing grace toward my husband.

When you bake a cake, the measurements must be exact. If the recipe calls for a quarter cup, then you fill that quarter cup with just enough flour. Not too much, not too little. Thankfully, God's love is in no way based on exact measurements. God's love never comes in a "just enough" size. His love doesn't just fit; it's overflowing and incomprehensibly more than we can imagine or deserve. In the book of Philemon, we witness this kind of grace demonstrated beautifully. A slave named Onesimus had run away to Rome, and by divine Providence, he met the apostle Paul and subsequently came to faith. But there remained a problem: Most commentators believe Onesimus had stolen from his master or wronged him in some way, and thus he had a debt to repay. So Paul wrote to Philemon, a wealthy businessman and member of the Colossian church. Paul appealed to him on behalf of Onesimus. In his appeal, Paul asks Philemon to accept Onesimus back not as a slave but as a brother in Christ. He further urges Philemon to forgive Onesimus for any wrong-doing and even tells him that he, Paul, will pay any debt himself. This was more love, more mercy than Onesimus may have deserved, but it is a powerful demonstration of grace.

God wants us to love in this unconditional way too. His love is abundant, and because we have experienced it, we can turn around and give the same love to others. But how do we get there? When we have been wronged, how do we forgive and love with abandon? It starts and ends with understanding God's grace. When we grasp just how undeserving of God's love and grace we are, we are then in a place to be able to extend grace to others and really love them without resentment.

In the book of Philemon, we see Paul call Philemon to a love that is unconditional. He is calling not for a love based on human performance but for an extravagant love based on forgiveness and grace. The story of Philemon and Onesimus is relatable to any of us because it demonstrates gospel hope for any relationship. No matter what separates us—the wrongs we have done or the wrongs done against us—the grace of God is powerful enough to foster reconciliation. Philemon is the shortest of Paul's letters, but it's oh-so-full of grace. Paul urges and appeals to Philemon as a brother in Christ. He asks him to consider Onesimus based on Christian love for him. Paul uses the Greek word *koinonia* (1:6), which means "partnership," "fellowship," or "participation,"[1] to appeal to Philemon to forgive Onesimus, reminding Philemon that our participation in the gospel gives us equal standing in front of Christ. This word signifies our bond as believers and how we live a shared life in Christ. Under the laws of the time, Onesimus deserved punishment, but Paul asks Philemon to restore and forgive him.

The truth is, none of us deserve love like that. Our ability to love, to be sanctified, and to have faith are all gifts. As Ephesians 2:8 puts it, "For by grace you have been saved through faith. And this is not your own doing; it is the gift of God" (ESV).

Receive the gift, and in turn give the gift of love to others—a heaping cup of it.

The truth of the gospel changes us and, as a result, changes our relationships.

When we are able to forgive, it is a great testimony to the gracious work of our own heavenly Father. How could a holy God love people who are so far from being holy on their own? Because we are His creation and He created us to be in relationship with Him. He loves us so much that He sent His Son, Jesus Christ, to pay our debt. If this gospel of grace can transform Philemon and Onesimus into brothers in Christ, it can also transform us. God will no longer see us as sinners but as sisters and brothers of Christ.

I love what one commentator said about the "persuasive power" of the letter of Philemon: "Not without reason, when compared with the Letter to the Philippians, it is asserted that Paul there appears as the 'Christian saint,' but here as the 'Christian gentleman.' A painful matter to the runaway Onesimus is here put right for him by Paul in a short Letter in which his greatness of soul is apparent in the gentle and humane tenderness, tact, and persuasive power without command or compulsion. The love which constrains him is worthy of admiration, as well as the wisdom which guides him. The Letter is a testimony to the sanctified 'art of treating people' in which Paul excels."[2]

As a reminder, here are the background questions we ask before reading a book of the Bible. Let's answer each one on the book of Philemon:

- Which book am I studying?
- Who wrote the book?
- To whom was it written?
- Where was it written?

- When was the book written?
- What is the literary genre?

A Note on Slavery

When reading the book of Philemon, we would be remiss not to acknowledge the elephant in the room: slavery. It is right for us as believers to be concerned about this. Why does Paul not call for the abolishment of slavery? Why does he not stand against such a perverse institution? Many people will read this book and find it alarming that Paul does not call for outright social reform. Where is his plea for Onesimus's release? I have included below a perspective from one of my favorite commentaries to answer this question for us.

> For many, Paul moved too slowly in abolishing an evil institution. However, we must remember that the early church lived in its own context. While slavery was generally accepted, many voices spoke against it during the first century. Some of these incited riots. Paul knew that the church could not be perceived as the instigator of rebellion leading to loss of life. The Roman Empire had within it the mechanism for effecting change, and that change had to come voluntarily from the individuals whose lives were changed by their Lord. Slaves could be freed by anyone, even if their freedom at times caused more problems than it solved. Paul chose the theological route. If the theological seed were sown, a solid foundation existed for a permanent change that was more socially pervasive than one institution. Paul taught equality. Slaves served Christ in spite of their economic situation. Their owners were also slaves, only they were slaves to the Master in heaven. This equality was to lead the way to sympathy for one another. Further, God called people to serve Him in varied circumstances, and He judged impartially. The application of these principles would bring a de facto end to the institution.[3]

Day One

Read all of Philemon.

Focus Verses

Philemon 1:1-7

Observation

1. Highlight or list all the names mentioned in this passage.

   _____

   _____

   _____

2. Read this verse in three different translations. Does comparing
   translations help you understand the passage more broadly or
   internalize it differently? What are some differences in the word
   choices the translators made?

   _____

   _____

   _____

   _____

Interpretation

Verse 1: In nine out of his thirteen letters, Paul calls himself an apostle when he introduces himself. Typically, his designation as an apostle shows he is going to deal with more theological themes. He also will often introduce himself as either a slave or servant. It is unique for him to introduce himself as a prisoner of Christ Jesus as he does at the start of Philemon. This designation helps us to see that this is a more personal letter, where Paul has begun to self-identify with the suffering of the gospel. In drawing our attention to this designation as prisoner, he invokes sympathy and points us to his loyalty and submission to Christ in all things.

Paul wrote this letter to Philemon, a "dear friend and fellow worker." Philemon was a wealthy slave owner living in Colossae who hosted the church in his house. He likely became a believer under Paul's ministry. In this verse, Paul also mentions Timothy, who must have participated in some way in sending the letter to Philemon.

Verse 2: Apphia's identity is unknown, but she may have been Philemon's wife.[4]

Verse 3: Paul includes salutations here: grace and peace. Grace and peace are customary greetings that Paul often uses. Grace is always mentioned before peace, as grace is the bedrock of peace. We can only have peace when we receive God's grace, thereby allowing us to give grace to others and receive peace in human relationships. These salutations point toward two of the themes we will see in this letter.

Verses 4-5: Paul thanks God for Philemon whenever he remembers him in prayer. Paul knew about Philemon's love and faith. Paul knew he could speak with Philemon about a difficult subject because of their relationship and shared faith. Let's be willing to confront others—and to receive correction from them—especially when we share faith in Christ.

Verses 6-7: Paul urges Philemon to consider their shared partnership in Christ. He uses the Greek word *koinonia* to explain that they are all mutual benefactors of the gospel, in hopes that this truth would inform Philemon's forgiveness of Onesimus.

Philemon's love has encouraged Paul and has refreshed the hearts of the Lord's people. A great way to bring refreshment is to pray over others who are struggling.

Application

1. Think of the last time a Christian friend or family member confronted you. How did the conversation go? Did you learn anything from it that you can apply in the future?

   _____

   _____

   _____

   _____

   _____

2. How can you seek to refresh those around you with love and encouragement? Think of one actionable way you can do that this week.

   _____

   _____

   _____

   _____

   _____

Space for Reflection

Day Two

Focus Verses

Philemon 1:8-11

Observation

1. Highlight or list any repeated words in this passage.

   _____

   _____

2. What does Onesimus's name mean? Look it up in your study Bible
   or a commentary.

   _____

   _____

Interpretation

Verses 8-9: Paul could use his apostolic authority to command Philemon
to do what he says, but instead he appeals to him in love. Based on their
shared faith and commonality, Philemon ought to extend forgiveness. This

principle should work its way out in all of our lives. Most generous is a man who does not demand out of his own authority but gently persuades another. We can take note of how Paul approaches Philemon with respect as he tries to persuade him to pardon Onesimus. He does so from love, based on their shared faith. It is wise that when we desire to convince someone that we would appeal to them based on what we know they believe. "He wants Philemon to act out of conviction, not out of compulsion."[5]

In parenting, we might try to coerce our children into feeling convicted, but we cannot feel convicted for them. The best thing we can do is continually remind them of what the Bible says and of their identity in Christ.

Verse 10: Paul had gotten to know Onesimus while he was in chains in Rome, and Onesimus became a friend and a brother in Christ. Onesimus had fled his master, Philemon, running from Colossae all the way to Rome, where somehow he had come into contact with Paul, who led him to Christ. Throughout this book, it is obvious that divine Providence brought Onesimus into Paul's company after he ran away.

Verse 11: This is a play on words by Paul because the name Onesimus means "useful." Onesimus became useful in God's Kingdom at the moment he trusted in Jesus. We all desire to be seen as useful and live useful lives. Yet when God gets hold of us and we are regenerated, we automatically become useful. It is God working in us that makes us useful. He is the One who causes growth.

Application

1. Think of someone in your life whose behavior is not Christlike. How could you talk to them about their actions out of love?

2. When was the last time you tried to be useful?

_____

_____

_____

I encourage you to turn over this desire to Christ. He knows of your desire, and He cares. Pray this prayer with me:

Lord God,

I so desire to be useful. When my life feels like it doesn't have purpose or I am circling, frustrated, and inept, remind me that it is You who makes us useful—it is not of my own doing. I pray that every day would be one I could commit to being useful to You.

Space for Reflection

_____

_____

_____

_____

_____

_____

_____

_____

_____

Focus Verses

Philemon 1:12-16

Verse 16 contains a contrast: "no longer as a slave, but . . . as a dear brother." To read more about contrasts and comparisons in Scripture, turn to page 127 of Chasing Sacred.

Observation

1. What does the phrase "who is my very heart" lead you to infer about Paul and Onesimus's relationship?

   _____

   _____

2. What is the explanation that Paul gives for Philemon and Onesimus being separated from each other?

   _____

   _____

   _____

Interpretation

Verses 12-14: Paul appeals to Philemon and asks him to forgive Onesimus. Paul is sending Onesimus back to his master with the hopes that Philemon will show him grace. It is beautiful to see the way Paul talks to Philemon. As one commentator says, "Compulsion, constraint, coercion, necessity, and so forth are not the attitudes out of which a person is to serve Christ. God loves one who gives gladly, 'not reluctantly or under compulsion' (2 Cor. 9:7). Philemon will best reveal his true Christian character when he acts voluntarily."[6]

It is difficult to remind ourselves that heart change must be voluntary, not demanded. I experience this most often in parenting. It feels easier to get our kids to behave externally than to change their hearts. Sin can play dress-up, but sin is truly about the heart. Whether it's your spouse's anger, your jealousy, or someone's unloving, subtle digs, it's all sin. An explosive and blatant outburst is no worse than a toxic heart posture, and we need to remember that in order to be able to extend grace and disciple others.

In the parenting book *Give Them Grace*, authors Elyse Fitzpatrick and Jessica Thompson point out that the same sin in your spunky, rule-breaking kid is also in the heart of your rule-following child: "The children who actually end up performing better are those who understand that their relationship with God doesn't depend on their performance for Jesus but on Jesus' performance for them. With the right mixture of fear and guilt, I can get my three children to obey in the short term. But my desire is not that they obey for five minutes or even for five days. My desire is that they obey for fifty years!"[7]

Verse 15: This verse so beautifully illustrates God's sovereign hand over the lives of Onesimus and Philemon. Onesimus found his way to Paul, became saved, and returned to his master. All believers find themselves in situations where they have made a wrong decision. But by God's providence and forgiveness, He even allows our mess-ups to become part of His grand story of redemption. If you feel that your steps are not ordained, look no further than the story of Philemon and Onesimus to find comfort in God's intentionality with all the events of your life.

Verse 16: We see a beautiful exchange here, as detailed by Paul. Onesimus is no longer a slave but rather a brother in Christ. We all must make this shift in our perspective on other believers. Even those who were once our enemies have become our brothers and sisters in Christ. If the people you are dealing with are fellow believers, then before your husband became your husband, and before your friend became your friend, and before your enemy became your enemy, he or she was your brother in Christ.

If your enemy is in Christ, he or she was first your *sibling*. The church is God's family, unified under the Trinity. As we operate as a church family under our relational God, we can accept that those around us are closer to us than our flesh and blood. We are all one by the power of His blood.

How do you typically treat your siblings? To me, my sister and brother can do no wrong. When someone messes with my siblings, my inner boxer comes out to defend and uphold their character. If they need space, I give it to them. If they are going through something, I understand. They are my siblings; I will defend them and go to bat for them, always. I understand this explanation might not be helpful if you have a difficult relationship with your siblings. If that's the case, think of your best friend instead. As Romans 15:7 says, "Accept one another, then, just as Christ accepted you, in order to bring praise to God." Why would we hold our spouses and friends to a different standard than we do our siblings?

Application

1. Write down one relationship where you could experience freedom if you treated the person more like a sibling in Christ than an enemy. Whom do you need to make this shift with?

_____

_____

_____

2. When you were growing up, was heart change or behavior change emphasized more?

_____

_____

Space for Reflection

_____
_____
_____
_____
_____
_____
_____
_____
_____
_____
_____
_____
_____
_____
_____
_____
_____

Focus Verses

Philemon 1:17-21

Observation

1. Where do we see Paul making a personal appeal to Philemon in these verses?

_____

_____

_____

_____

2. In your own words, paraphrase what Paul is saying in these verses.

_____

_____

_____

_____

Interpretation

Verse 17: Paul continually reminds Philemon of their relationship—for instance, "if you consider me a partner." He reminds Philemon that they are partners in the gospel. In any difficult relationship with another Christian, we need to be reminded of the person's connection with us through Christ. It is easy to demonize or ostracize someone if you forget that you are "one body" (1 Corinthians 12:12), that you are on the same team.

Verses 18-19: Paul tells Philemon that he will pay any debt Onesimus owes. This resembles the gospel story so beautifully. I love how one commentator explains it:

> In this magnificent section of Scripture, one final truth emerges. Paul served as the agent of reconciliation. Perhaps in his mind his relationship to Christ demanded it. There is no better picture of what Jesus did for humanity than what Paul did and offered to do for Onesimus. He brought the offender to a point of reconciliation, and he embodied that reconciliation since both parties were intimately related to him. Paul practiced the mind of Christ in everyday relationships. His study of Jesus' role in reconciliation of persons and God no doubt taught about reconciliation. Further, his service to Christ motivated him to reconcile persons to God and to each other. Christ demands this type of humble, Christlike service.[8]

Verses 20-21: Paul has perfected the art of calling up instead of out. He calls Philemon up by reminding him of his obedience to Christ first and foremost. Telling Philemon that he is confident he will do even more than he asks shows that Paul puts great faith in Philemon. When you establish your love for someone, hard requests can follow. When you focus on your commonality and do not dwell on your differences, reconciliation may be less difficult.

Application

1. In your own words, write how Paul, Onesimus, and Philemon's story resembles the gospel.

_____

_____

_____

_____

2. Write down the names of a few people who refresh your heart in Christ, and take some time to thank God for them today.

_____

_____

_____

Space for Reflection

_____

_____

_____

_____

_____

_____

_____

_____

_____

_____

_____

be strengthened with all his glorious power so you will have all the endurance
eed. May you be filled with joy, 12 always thanking the Father. He has enabled
e inheritance that belongs to his people, who live in the light. 13 For he has re
ingdom of darkness and transferred us into the Kingdom of his dear Son, 14 who
om and forgave our sins. 15 Christ is the visible image of the invisible God. He
ing was created and is supreme over all creation. 16 for through him God create
e heavenly realms and on   e can see and the things w
as thrones, kingdoms, rul   nseen world. Everything
gh him and for him. 17 He   se, and he holds all creati
t is also the head of the   e is the beginning, suprem
rom the dead. So he is first in everything. 19 For God in all his fullness was p
ist, 20 and through him God reconciled everything to himself. He made peace w
aven and on earth by means of Christ's blood on the cross. 21 This includes you

Day Five

Focus Verses

Philemon 1:22-25

Observation

1. Highlight or list all the verbs in this passage.

2. Highlight or list all the names that are mentioned.

Interpretation

Verse 22: We do not know if Philemon followed through and freed Onesimus from slavery and debt. But observing this letter we see that Paul was pretty confident he would, based on Philemon's character. Paul was so trusting of Philemon that he was comfortable telling Philemon he'd be staying in his home. Our character should be so evident that when someone speaks against us, our character gives reason for others to doubt the integrity of the slander. The end result of this letter is now known to Philemon, Paul, Onesimus, and the Lord.

Verses 23-25: The ministry partners mentioned in this last farewell are some of the same people listed in Colossians, which indicates the book of Philemon was written around the same time. Paul ends the letter with a benediction of God's grace.

Application

End this time of your study of Philemon by asking yourself a few questions:

1. Is there a debt that God is asking you to release someone from? Do you feel convicted of resentment or bitterness that you have been holding on to? What principles from this study of Philemon can help you to forgive?

_____

_____

_____

_____

_____

_____

2. In what ways does the gospel free you to see other brothers and sisters in Christ in a different manner?

_____

_____

_____

3. **Philemon is a small but mighty book.** What is your main takeaway from this book?

_____

_____

_____

Space for Reflection

_____

_____

_____

_____

_____

_____

_____

_____

_____

_____

_____

_____

_____

_____

Lord God,

I thank You for the power You have to transform human relationships. Thank You that no relationship is past the point of reconciliation or repair if You are working in and through it. I pray for the difficult relationships in my life. Grant me the grace to persist, the discernment to set necessary boundaries, and the strength to transform these relationships. In moments where forgiveness feels beyond my reach, strengthen me with Your divine power to forgive the unforgivable and to heal where healing seems impossible.

Thank You, Lord.

In Jesus' name, amen.

Final Thoughts

i we give thanks to God, the Father of our Lord Jesus Christ. 4 For we have heard
Christ Jesus and your love for all of God's people, 5 which come from your confi
God has reserved for you in heaven. You have had this expectation ever since yo
he truth of the Good News. 6 This same Good News that came to you is going out a
t is bearing fruit everywhere by changing lives, just as it changed your lives f
st heard and understood the truth about God's wonderful grace. 7 You learned ab
om Epaphras, our beloved co-worker. He is Christ's faithful servant, and he is h
behalf. 8 He has told us about the love for others that the Holy Spirit has give
not stopped praying for you since we first heard about you. We ask God to give
lge of his will and to give you spiritual wisdom and understanding. 10 Then the
11 always honor and please the Lord, and your lives will produce every kind of
while, you will grow as you learn to know God better and better. 11 We also pray
strengthened with all his glorious power so you will have all the endurance a
d. May you be filled with joy, 12 always thanking the Father. He has enabled yo
nheritance that belongs to his people, who live in the light. 13 For he has resc
gdom of darkness and transferred us into the Kingdom of his dear Son, 14 who pu
n and forgave our sins. 15 Christ is the visible image of the invisible God. He ex
g was created and is supreme over all creation, 16 for through him God created
eavenly realms and on earth. He made the things we can see and the things we c
thrones, kingdoms, rulers, and authorities in the unseen world. Everything wa
n him and for him. 17 He existed before anything else, and he holds all creation
is also the head of the church, which is his body. He is the beginning, supreme
om the dead. So he is first in everything. 19 For God in all his fullness was ple
st, 20 and through him God reconciled everything to himself. He made peace wi
en and on earth by means of Christ's blood on the cross. 21 This includes you wh
y from God. You were his enemies, separated from him by your evil thoughts and
low he has reconciled you to himself through the death of Christ in his physic
t, he has brought you into his own presence, and you are holy and blameless as
him without a single fault. 23 But you must continue to believe this truth and
on't drift away from the assurance you received when you heard the Good News.
is been preached all over the world, and I, Paul, have been appointed as God's s
m it. 24 I am glad when I suffer for you in my body, for I am participating in th
st that continue for his body, the church. 25 God has given me the responsibilit
rch by proclaiming his entire message to you. 26 This message was kept secret
erations past, but now it has been revealed to God's people. 27 For God wanted

be strengthened with all his glorious power so you will have all the endurance
eed. May you be filled with joy, 12 always thanking the Father. He has enabled
e inheritance that belongs to his people, who live in the light. 13 For he has re
ingdom of darkness and transferred us into the Kingdom of his dear Son, 14 who
iom and forgave our sins. 15 Christ is the visible image of the invisible God. He
ning was created and is supreme over all creation, 16 for through him God create
e heavenly re   the things w
as thrones, k   . Everything
igh him and f   lds all creati
st is also the head of the church, which is his body. He is the beginning, suprem
from the dead. So he is first in everything. 19 For God in all his fullness was
rist, 20 and through him God reconciled everything to himself. He made peace

Letter from the Author

FRIENDS, RECENTLY I'VE BEEN DRAWN TO the idea of a see-through purse. Just the other day, I spotted the most adorable translucent shoulder bag. I debated over this purchase for a while, only to realize that no one really wants to see everything inside my purse. Currently, there's makeup smudged on the sides, a bit of trash, crumpled receipts, and even a ballpoint pen that's left its mark inside. And let's not forget the diapers, baby food, and an old spoon.

Colossians and Philemon can be likened to such see-through purses. They aren't like those curated social media accounts that showcase only the highlights. Instead, they offer genuine reflections of what's inside our hearts. Colossians pushes us to dedicate ourselves entirely to Christ, suggesting that every aspect of our lives should be as transparent as a see-through purse. It encourages us to uphold morality in private and ensure that our outward behavior mirrors our inner virtues, such as gentleness and self-control. Colossians urges us to see how our union with Christ—and Christ's work on our behalf—is the impetus to change.

Philemon, on the other hand, nudges us to cultivate the ability to forgive, to maintain peace with others, and to support and uplift those in our God-given relationships.

It's crucial for us to deeply trust God's ability to mold us and our fellow believers. We must be so convinced by the transformative power of the Spirit's work in our lives and the reading of God's Word that our beliefs and actions align. In Colossians, we learn that doctrinal truths can inspire genuine change in our hearts. Meanwhile, Philemon illustrates how our newfound identity as heavenly citizens can rejuvenate and transform our relationships. The challenge lies in resisting the pull of sin and ensuring that no aspect of our lives remains hidden from Christ or ourselves. While we might repeatedly fall and rise, true freedom in Christ allows us to be introspective about what God has done on our behalf and proudly declare that our lives are as transparent as a see-through purse.

When we stand righteous before the Lord, understanding it is because of what He did for us on the cross, we can approach Him with unwavering confidence. Ultimate freedom lies in being liberated from the chains of sin and death. Our faith isn't in our mere human capabilities, but in God's promise that He listens to the prayers of the righteous, extends His protection, showcases His might in our lives, and is constantly guiding us from one glory to the next. May we be confident that because of what He did, we can become who He has planned for us to be.

Interpreting the Epistles

THERE ARE TWENTY-ONE EPISTLES (LETTERS) in the New Testament, many of them authored by Paul. The audience for the Epistles varies; some are written to individuals, some to communities, and some were intended for multiple churches. The Epistles were written for a variety of purposes: for example, to address different issues or problems, such as sinful behavior and disunity, or to provide encouragement to a church facing hardship or persecution. We must read the Epistles as history but also recognize their relevance for us today.

Interpreting Colossians

We know that the book of Colossians was originally a letter, which means we should keep in mind the original author and recipients of the letter. Remember, there were no chapter breaks or headings in the original letter. Remembering this will help you as you seek to understand the letter as a whole, following the themes and main ideas throughout the entirety of the epistle.

Paul wrote some of his letters to encourage or uplift a body of believers. Usually you can observe whether he was friendly with the churches or had heard from someone about what was going on. In the introduction to his letter to the Colossians, Paul writes, "Since we heard of your faith in Christ

Jesus and the love which you have for all the saints" (1:4, NASB). Whom did Paul hear this from? "From Epaphras, our dear fellow servant, who is a faithful minister of Christ on our behalf, and who also told us of your love in the Spirit" (1:7-8).

As one commentator explains, the beginning of a letter from Bible times often contains three elements: "the name of the sender or senders, the name of the addressee or addressees, and a message of greeting. The greeting used habitually by Jews was 'Peace!' (Heb. shālôm) or, more fully, 'Mercy and peace!' . . . The form 'grace and peace' is characteristically Pauline: both terms have their full Christian force."[1]

Many of Paul's epistles are known for his strong defense of the gospel against certain problems within a specific church. Although we want to reconstruct the information as much as possible, we also want to balance this by leaving out what was meant to be left out. If the Bible does not contain certain things and we are left speculating, we do not want to speculate so far as to add to Scripture.

Appendix B

Tracing the Theme of Chaos vs. Order

MY RICKETY OLD SCHOOL IN THAILAND received at least thirty new
students in what felt like minutes. Soon enough, I had a plethora of new
friend choices. The sad part was that this had all resulted from a sudden
attack on a school in Pakistan. I can only imagine the terror the kids experienced at the school when they were attacked by an outsider. Several guards
and staff were killed as the children waited with bated breath inside. The
trauma was unthinkable.

It quickly became evident that it was too dangerous for these children
of missionaries to live in the hills of Pakistan. The entire school moved to
Chiang Mai, Thailand, to join ours. A couple of these students became
some of my closest friends. One was Canadian and the other was Pakistani,
both joyful additions to my life.

One of my new friends told me a story that still haunts me to this day.
I remember her sharing it with me, remorse in her eyes. "It was my fault,"
she whispered one night at a sleepover. I listened intently as she disclosed
one of her most painful memories. She was swimming with her family in
a rough-water zone when she began to drown. Unable to keep her head
above water, she flailed and began to sink. The water was swallowing her
whole, and at that moment, her uncle made a choice. He jumped into the
water to save her. He hoisted her up onto the boat, but he, too, began to

be taken by the current. He was swept underwater, and the current took him down. Her uncle lost his life that day. It was not her fault, as we can all recognize. Her uncle chose to save her that day—despite the danger. When I think about this story, I thank Jesus for jumping into the chaotic waters to save us.

Jesus' incarnation meant He became flesh and dwelled among us. Through Jesus' sacrificial death on the cross, He entered chaos, made sense of our world, and brought wholeness from the disorder that sin caused. Although my friend's uncle reminds me of Christ, Christ's story has significant differences. He not only jumped into chaos with us but conquered it. He rose above it, overcame, and is Lord over it.

Throughout *Chasing Sacred* and this Bible study, I have subtly pointed to the theme of chaos and order. The reason I have done this is to show how one overarching theme can fit into the metanarrative of Scripture. I wanted to demonstrate how one theme can be found throughout the Bible from Genesis to Revelation. I do not want you to just take my word for it. I want to teach you how to search for biblical themes throughout the Bible's pages.

In the beginning, God's spoken Word filled the formless void. Only chaos exists until God speaks. Did you get that? Your life might feel purposeless, but it is not. It has purpose because God *speaks*. What happens when God speaks into this chaos? He orders it. God shows rhythmic dependability, stability, and peace; as the day turns to night repeatedly, God creates time and orders all that exists through His Word. The Word of God is the antidote to confusion. This is equally true in our culture of confusion today. God's Word is the clarity in our midst.

When I was a new mother, no matter how hard I tried, life felt chaotic, and over the years I have struggled with many periods of deep confusion in motherhood, marriage, and ministry. Just as in the Creation account, God's Word continually brings order and life amid those struggles. When a season of depression smacked me in the face, I felt that the only truth I could cling to was in His Word. *Why did God put me here, and what is the purpose of my existence?* I went time and time again back to His Word.

Through the prophet Isaiah, God makes a promise. He says, "So shall My word be that goes forth from My mouth; it shall not return to Me void, but it shall accomplish what I please, and it shall prosper in the thing for which I sent it" (Isaiah 55:11, NKJV). What a promise! His Word will not return void. He accomplishes His purposes in our lives through His Word. His Word that came out of His mouth at the beginning of time accomplished what He desired: a created, beautiful, ordered world (see John 1:1-3). The consistent practice that brought both meaning and order to my life was reading the Scriptures, studying them, and applying them. All of these disciplines brought so much clarity to my life. God was ordering my world more and more for His purposes and His honor through His Word.

From Genesis to Revelation

Chaos and order is a great example of a theme that we see not only in Colossians but in the whole Bible. When we study Colossians, or any book of the Bible, it is important to also consider whether the book has themes that resonate throughout Scripture.

In searching for the theme of chaos and order, I began with both books, Genesis and Revelation. (Nancy Guthrie also recommends this.) Searching for themes in the bookends of Scripture has proved helpful for me as a study. Tracing a theme immediately from Genesis all the way to Revelation may seem overwhelming. Instead, I personally found it helpful to begin with both Genesis and Revelation and to see how the fulfillment of what was promised in Genesis comes to fruition in Revelation. In both books, we see watery chaos. We see that God is Lord over all that chaos in the very beginning of time, and we see how He orders it by the very act of creation. God conquers and reigns over the chaos described in Revelation—He shows Himself victorious over it all. Revelation is the culmination of chaos being restored back to its original order. "He will wipe every tear from their eyes. There will be no more death or mourning or crying or pain, for the old order of things has passed away" (Revelation 21:4).

While you don't have to study the Bible exactly the way I do, I think it can be helpful to unpack a theme by starting with Genesis and Revelation. Now let's move from Genesis to Exodus to seek out the theme of chaos and order.

Exodus

The theme of chaos and order is woven throughout the book of Exodus. At many points in the narrative, we notice the presence of chaos. The Israelites' slavery under Pharaoh was not how God has ordered and designed for His people to be in relationship to Him. The Hebrew words used in these narratives link the crossing of the Red Sea's chaotic waters to the Creation account. But we also see the theme of order. God restores His people into proper relationship with Himself, freeing them from slavery and establishing orderly communal life for them through the giving of His law.

When we think about chaos, many of us flash to memories of our kitchens in disorder or to a time when our emotions felt out of sync. The first thing we try and do is to order these things *ourselves*. If you are anything like me, you might take your stress out on your children. When I scream at them to help me get my house out of its dysfunctional state, I feel like I am doing something. I harp on them and try to control the situation because parts of my life feel so out of my control.

Do I think that our desire to create order and peace is a good one? Absolutely. We are made in God's image. However, if we feel the need to control every single thing, we are trying to play God. Pharaoh is like this in Exodus: he tries to control God's people and be a god himself. Pharaoh ends up participating in the chaos instead of actually ordering anything. His stubborn refusal to give up his control to God produces even more chaos and the plagues keep on coming.

God administers judgment in the form of these chaotic plagues to show where our faith and trust are to be placed: not in our own control, but in God's control and order of the cosmos. The plagues point to the fact that the Lord is the only One who wields power to control the natural world. The Egyptian gods could not affect the natural world—only God can. God is completely in control of creation and of what happens to His people.

After using chaos to judge Egypt, the Lord provides a way through the chaos of the Red Sea and gives the Israelites the moral law on Mount Sinai. The Ten Commandments demonstrate God's will for His people to live lives of order, not chaos. God's laws show us what God loves and what

God hates. He doesn't want order for order's sake; He brings order out of love and concern for His people. True life is only found in knowing Him and living life in the order that He creates and desires for us.

Job

The theme of chaos and order is explicit in the book of Job. We find out in the beginning chapters that Job is a man who "feared God and shunned evil" (1:1). Satan is allowed to bring chaos to Job's life, though God puts bounds and limits on the evil that Satan is allowed to unleash on Job. Although Job curses the day he was born, he does not curse God in the midst of his trials.

Later in the book of Job, we see God asking Job about the sea monster Leviathan. "Can you pull in Leviathan with a fishhook or tie down its tongue with a rope?" (41:1) Leviathan represents chaos: "In ancient pagan myths Leviathan was a sea monster that inhabited 'the deep,' the chaotic waters. It was 'a repressive, anti-creation monster who swallow[ed] up life.'"[1] God's command of Leviathan shows that He rules over even the primeval deep. He demonstrates this to Job by reminding him of the Creation account and who orders the world:

> Where were you when I laid the earth's foundation?
>   Tell me, if you understand.
> Who marked off its dimensions? Surely you know!
>   Who stretched a measuring line across it? . . .
>
> Who shut up the sea behind doors . . .
> when I fixed limits for it
>   and set its doors and bars in place,
> when I said, "This far you may come and no farther;
>   here is where your proud waves halt"?
>
> Have you ever given orders to the morning,
>   or shown the dawn its place?

JOB 38:4-5, 8, 10-12

CHASING SACRED BIBLE STUDY

God reminds Job of His divine attributes: His sovereignty, His intentionality, His creative order. In the end, God restores Job's life to order: "The LORD restored his fortunes and gave him twice as much as he had before" (42:10).

Psalms

We also see the theme of chaos and order present in the Psalms: for example, in Psalm 148. The emphasis in this psalm is how God rules over creation, and that even the chaotic "sea creatures" and "stormy winds" praise the Lord (verses 7-8). This points us toward the fact that God controls all things, and He is Lord and King. His purposes will prevail.

Jeremiah

Jeremiah uses creation language to describe the coming punishment and destruction of Judah and Jerusalem because of all their sins. As a matter of fact, he describes it as a reversal of creation. Genesis 1:1-2 says that God created the *tohu wabohu*, that is, formless and empty matter. Then God took this unformed, chaotic blob and shaped creation out of it. We see this same phrase in Jeremiah:

> I looked at the earth, and it was empty and formless.
> I looked at the heavens, and there was no light.
> I looked at the mountains and hills,
> and they trembled and shook.
> I looked, and all the people were gone.
> All the birds of the sky had flown away.
> I looked, and the fertile fields had become a wilderness.
> The towns lay in ruins,
> crushed by the LORD's fierce anger.
>
> JEREMIAH 4:23-26, NLT

Sin reverses the order of creation. As a result, God basically says that He is going back to square one. God always preserves His people and provides hope in the midst of judgment. This thought of decreation is carried further when Jeremiah says that the light (presumably the sun, moon, and stars created on the fourth day) of heaven is going to go out. Furthermore, the mountains, which are the height of stability, will actually begin quaking and swaying. Jeremiah then turns to the animate part of creation, and we see that people and birds are gone. The land turns into a desert. As one scholar puts it, "The dissolution of Judah is itself an undoing of creation."[2]

The Gospels

In chapter 3 of *Chasing Sacred*, I write about being spared from having to search for my kids' pacifiers in a desperate attempt to soothe them—and the amazing invention of the glow-in-the-dark pacifier. This story has often served as an analogy for me when searching through the pages of Scripture for answers to a theological question or an issue in my Christian walk. When we flip through the pages of the Bible, we want to find the glowing pacifier, the beaming hope of a weary world: Christ.

We would be remiss not to point out how the theme of chaos and order finds its culmination in Christ. All of Scripture points to the Kingdom of God and is fulfilled in the rule and reign of Jesus. It shows us how we can enter into His Kingdom, a Kingdom void of chaos and darkness. A Kingdom with a perfect King.

When we search for the theme of chaos and order in the Gospels, we see Jesus restoring wholeness to creation. He came as the Light of the World (see John 8:12). Darkness is chaotic, but the light that shines amid the chaos is Jesus. Darkness obscures our path, but when Jesus—the Light of the World—came, He said, "I have come into the world as a light, so that no one who believes in me should stay in darkness" (John 12:46). To follow the way of Jesus means to follow the light and to shine as children of light.

Throughout Scripture, God invites us into His restoration of order. We restore order to our homes and to our relationships when we speak truth.

We restore order to our lives when we read and apply the Scriptures. We restore order when we accept the invitation to participate in God's Kingdom. We see the order that God's Son, Jesus, brought to us on the Cross by restoring our relationship with Him. This restoration of order is a gift of grace, a grace that existed before time began, "which he gave us in Christ Jesus before the ages began" (2 Timothy 1:9, ESV). His saving grace, which we do not deserve, reconciles us with Him, and His enabling grace helps us to share in His creative order, to desire order in our lives, and to participate in restoring order to creation. God helps us do this through our spiritual gifts and assists us in helping those in need and keeping our priorities rightly ordered. The Holy Spirit is the power that fuels our ability to restore order. When we listen to the Spirit's direction, we are able to pursue order in our lives.

As John Barry and Rebecca Van Noord write, "Next time things seem to get rough, try replacing the cliché of 'God is in control' with 'God is Lord over chaos.' The tense here is important. God isn't *trying* to be Lord—He *is* Lord. When God spoke, the chaos was subdued. Likewise, when God speaks truth into our lives, the chaos in our lives is subdued. Through Christ's work, we can engage in this intimate relationship with God. Through Christ's efforts in us, we can become people who act with Him to subdue chaos. *What chaos do you need God to subdue today?*"[3]

I hope this study has demonstrated how incredibly rich the Scriptures are, with themes and threads running through the pages. They proclaim a unified message and make it clear how beautifully purposeful and intentional God is with His Word. It is incredible to see that we, too, can study it in a way where we can glean overarching ideas and themes throughout its pages. I hope you close this study saying, "I can do that!"

I do not think it is an accident that God repeatedly calms the chaos and restores order in the Bible. The point is not to focus on the order and the chaos in and of themselves, but to fix our eyes on the One who controls the chaos and restores order. When I began writing this book, my friend asked me, "Is chaos bad?" I would have given her a completely different response than I would now. When she asked me that question, I thought that maybe chaos was neutral with some bad elements in it, but that we could seek to control it. Now, I would let her know that chaos forces us to rely on Christ through petition, prayer, and Bible reading. Although sin wreaks havoc and has horrible consequences, the conviction of sin pushes us toward a prayerful life. It pushes us to acknowledge the true King of the Kingdom.

we give thanks to God, the Father of our Lord Jesus Christ. 4 For we have heard

Christ Jesus and your love for all of God's people, 5 which come from your confi

God has reserved for you in heaven. You have had this expectation ever since yo

e truth of the Good News. 6 This same Good News that came to you is going out al

t is bearing fruit everywhere by changing lives, just as it changed your lives fr

t heard and understood the truth about God's wonderful grace. 7 You learned ab

m Epaphras, our beloved co-worker. He is Christ's faithful servant, and he is h

behalf. 8 He has told us about the love for others that the Holy Spirit has give

not stopped praying for you since we first heard about you. We ask God to give y

ge of his will and to give you spiritual wisdom and understanding. 10 Then the

l always honor and please the Lord, and your lives will produce every kind of g

while, you will grow as you learn to know God better and better. 11 We also pray

strengthened with all his glorious power so you will have all the endurance an

. May you be filled with joy, 12 always thanking the Father. He has enabled you

heritance that belongs to his people, who live in the light. 13 For he has rescu

dom of darkness and transferred us into the Kingdom of his dear Son, 14 who pu

and forgave our sins. 15 Christ is the visible image of the invisible God. He ex

was created and is supreme over all creation, 16 for through him God created e

eavenly realms and on earth. He made the things we can see and the things we c

thrones, kingdoms, rulers, and authorities in the unseen world. Everything was

him and for him. 17 He existed before anything else, and he holds all creation

s also the head of the church, which is his body. He is the beginning, supreme

n the dead. So he is first in everything. 19 For God in all his fullness was ple

t, 20 and through him God reconciled everything to himself. He made peace with

n and on earth by means of Christ's blood on the cross. 21 This includes you who

from God. You were his enemies, separated from him by your evil thoughts and

w he has reconciled you to himself through the death of Christ in his physica

, he has brought you into his own presence, and you are holy and blameless as y

im without a single fault. 23 But you must continue to believe this truth and s

n't drift away from the assurance you received when you heard the Good News.

s been preached all over the world, and I, Paul, have been appointed as God's se

n it. 24 I am glad when I suffer for you in my body, for I am participating in the

t that continue for his body, the church. 25 God has given me the responsibility

ch by proclaiming his entire message to you. 26 This message was kept secret f

rations past, but now it has been revealed to God's people. 27 For God wanted t

Bible Study Resources

Ephesians, Colossians, Philemon by Arthur G. Patzia (Understanding
  the Bible Commentary Series)

Philippians, Colossians, Philemon by Richard R. Melick Jr. (The New
  American Commentary, volume 32)

The Epistles to the Colossians, to Philemon, and to the Ephesians by
  F. F. Bruce (The New International Commentary on the New
  Testament)

*Galatians, Ephesians, Philippians, Colossians, I and II Thessalonians,
  I and II Timothy, Titus, and Philemon* by George Whitefield Clark
  (Clark's Peoples Commentary)

Enduring Word (enduringword.com)

Blue Letter Bible (blueletterbible.org)

Bible Hub (biblehub.com)

we give thanks to God, the Father of our Lord Jesus Christ. 4 For we have heard

Christ Jesus and your love for all of God's people, 5 which come from your confi

God has reserved for you in heaven. You have had this expectation ever since yo

he truth of the Good News. 6 This same Good News that came to you is going out al

t is bearing fruit everywhere by changing lives, just as it changed your lives f

t heard and understood the truth about God's wonderful grace. 7 You learned ab

om Epaphras, our beloved co-worker. He is Christ's faithful servant, and he is h

behalf. 8 He has told us about the love for others that the Holy Spirit has given

not stopped praying for you since we first heard about you. We ask God to give y

ge of his will and to give you spiritual wisdom and understanding. 10 Then the

l always honor and please the Lord, and your lives will produce every kind of g

while, you will grow as you learn to know God better and better. 11 We also pray

strengthened with all his glorious power so you will have all the endurance an

l. May you be filled with joy, 12 always thanking the Father. He has enabled you

nheritance that belongs to his people, who live in the light. 13 For he has rescu

gdom of darkness and transferred us into the Kingdom of his dear Son, 14 who pu

and forgave our sins. 15 Christ is the visible image of the invisible God. He ex

g was created and is supreme over all creation, 16 for through him God created

eavenly realms and on earth. He made the things we can see and the things we c

thrones, kingdoms, rulers, and authorities in the unseen world. Everything wa

him and for him. 17 He existed before anything else, and he holds all creation

s also the head of the church, which is his body. He is the beginning, supreme

m the dead. So he is first in everything. 19 For God in all his fullness was ple

t, 20 and through him God reconciled everything to himself. He made peace wit

n and on earth by means of Christ's blood on the cross. 21 This includes you wh

from God. You were his enemies, separated from him by your evil thoughts and

ow he has reconciled you to himself through the death of Christ in his physica

, he has brought you into his own presence, and you are holy and blameless as y

im without a single fault. 23 But you must continue to believe this truth and s

n't drift away from the assurance you received when you heard the Good News. '

s been preached all over the world, and I, Paul, have been appointed as God's se

n it. 24 I am glad when I suffer for you in my body, for I am participating in the

t that continue for his body, the church. 25 God has given me the responsibility

rch by proclaiming his entire message to you. 26 This message was kept secret f

erations past, but now it has been revealed to God's people. 27 For God wanted t

Notes

INTRODUCTION

1. Arthur G. Patzia, *Ephesians, Colossians, Philemon*, Understanding the Bible Commentary Series (Grand Rapids, MI: Baker Books, 2011), 3.
2. Chuck Swindoll, "Colossians," Insight for Living Ministries, accessed October 20, 2023, https://insight.org/resources/bible/the-pauline-epistles/colossians.
3. Justin Taylor, "Six of My Favorite Quotes Luther Never Actually Said," The Gospel Coalition (TGC), February 20, 2014, https://www.thegospelcoalition.org/blogs /justin-taylor/5-quotes-that-luther-didnt-actually-say/.
4. Kevin DeYoung, *The Hole in Our Holiness: Filling the Gap between Gospel Passion and the Pursuit of Godliness* (Wheaton, IL: Crossway, 2012), 94.

WEEK ONE

1. Richard R. Melick Jr., *Philippians, Colossians, Philemon: An Exegetical and Theological Exposition of Holy Scripture*, The New American Commentary, vol. 32 (Nashville: B&H, 1991), 198–199.
2. Arthur G. Patzia, *Ephesians, Colossians, Philemon*, Understanding the Bible Commentary Series (Grand Rapids, MI: Baker Books, 2011), 22.
3. Sidney Greidanus, *From Chaos to Cosmos: Creation to New Creation* (Wheaton, IL: Crossway, 2018), 52.
4. Patzia, *Ephesians, Colossians, Philemon*, 23.
5. *ESV Gospel Transformation Study Bible* (Wheaton, IL: Crossway, 2019), study note on Colossians 1:24–2:5.
6. Elisabeth Elliot, *Keep a Quiet Heart* (Grand Rapids, MI: Fleming H. Revell, 2006), 20.

WEEK TWO

1. "6 Weird Facts about Your Body," *National Geographic*, January 5, 2017, YouTube video, 0:58, https://youtu.be/Crv0FtIruYk?si=K7tIZ1HY28VrzChw.

2. David Guzik, *Philippians and Colossians: Verse by Verse Commentary* (Enduring Word Media).

3. Ryan Morik, "Celtics Head Coach 'Only Familiar with' Jesus, Mary, and Joseph as Royal Family," Fox News, December 3, 2022, https://www.foxnews.com/sports /celtics-head-coach-only-familiar-jesus-mary-joseph-royal-family.

4. David Guzik, "Ephesians 2—God's Way of Reconciliation," Enduring Word, accessed October 24, 2023, https://enduringword.com/bible-commentary /ephesians-2.

5. Richard R. Melick Jr., *Philippians, Colossians, Philemon: An Exegetical and Theological Exposition of Holy Scripture*, The New American Commentary, vol. 32 (Nashville: B&H, 1991), 272.

WEEK THREE

1. Charles H. Spurgeon, *Morning and Evening: A New Edition of the Classic Devotional Based on the Holy Bible, English Standard Version*, revised and updated by Alistair Begg (Wheaton, IL: Crossway, 2003), 12.

2. *Life Application Study Bible*, 3rd ed. (Carol Stream, IL: Tyndale; Grand Rapids, MI: Zondervan, 2019), study note on Colossians 3:3.

3. William Barclay, "Commentary on Colossians 3," William Barclay's Daily Study Bible, StudyLight.org, accessed October 26, 2023, https://www.studylight .org/commentaries/eng/dsb/colossians-3.html.

4. David Guzik, "Colossians 3—Put Off, Put On," Enduring Word, accessed October 26, 2023, https://enduringword.com/bible-commentary/colossians-3/.

5. Biblehub.com, "anechó," accessed October 26, 2023, https://biblehub.com/greek /430.htm.

6. "Colossians 3:15 Commentary," Precept Austin, updated July 7, 2023, https://www.preceptaustin.org/colossians_315-16#3:15.

7. Richard R. Melick Jr., *Philippians, Colossians, Philemon: An Exegetical and Theological Exposition of Holy Scripture*, The New American Commentary, vol. 32 (Nashville: B&H, 1991), 311.

8. Melick, 315–316.

WEEK FOUR

1. Crystal Raypole, "How Many Thoughts Do You Have Each Day? And Other Things to Think About," Healthline, February 28, 2022, https://www.healthline .com/health/how-many-thoughts-per-day#thoughts-per-day; Prakhar Verma, "Destroy Negativity from Your Mind with This Simple Exercise," Medium, November 27, 2017, https://medium.com/the-mission/a-practical-hack-to -combat-negative-thoughts-in-2-minutes-or-less-cc3d1bddb3af.

2. Dallas Willard, "Personal Soul Care," DWillard.org, accessed October 27, 2023, https://dwillard.org/articles/personal-soul-care. Originally published in *The Pastors Guide to Effective Ministry* (Beacon Hill Press, 2002). Also available in *The Great Omission* (San Francisco: HarperCollins, 2006).

3. Charles H. Spurgeon, "A Sermon for the Week of Prayer" (sermon #354, London, January 7, 1861) in *The Complete Works of C. H. Spurgeon*, vol. 7 (Harrington, DE: Delmarva Publications, 2013).

4. F. F. Bruce, *The Epistles to the Colossians, to Philemon, and to the Ephesians*, The New International Commentary on the New Testament (Grand Rapids, MI: Eerdmans, 1984), 174.

5. Richard R. Melick Jr., *Philippians, Colossians, Philemon: An Exegetical and Theological Exposition of Holy Scripture*, The New American Commentary, vol. 32 (Nashville: B&H, 1991), 328.

WEEK FIVE

1. Biblehub.com, "koinónia," accessed October 29, 2023, https://biblehub.com/greek/2842.htm.

2. Jac J. Müller, *The Epistles of Paul to the Philippians and to Philemon: The English Text with Introduction, Exposition and Notes*, New International Commentary on the New Testament (Grand Rapids, MI: Eerdmans, 1955), 167.

3. Richard R. Melick Jr., *Philippians, Colossians, Philemon: An Exegetical and Theological Exposition of Holy Scripture*, The New American Commentary, vol. 32 (Nashville: B&H, 1991), 344.

4. Arthur G. Patzia, *Ephesians, Colossians, Philemon*, Understanding the Bible Commentary Series (Grand Rapids, MI: Baker Books, 2011), 106–107.

5. Patzia, 111.

6. Patzia, 112–113.

7. Elyse M. Fitzpatrick and Jessica Thompson, *Give Them Grace: Dazzling Your Kids with the Love of Jesus* (Wheaton, IL: Crossway, 2011).

8. Melick, *Philippians, Colossians, Philemon*, 367.

APPENDIX A

1. F. F. Bruce, *The Epistles to the Colossians, to Philemon, and to the Ephesians*, The New International Commentary on the New Testament (Grand Rapids, MI: Eerdmans, 1984), 39.

APPENDIX B

1. Sidney Greidanus, *From Chaos to Cosmos: Creation to New Creation* (Wheaton, IL: Crossway, 2018), 60.

2. John Goldingay, *Israel's Faith*, Old Testament Theology, vol. 2 (Downers Grove, IL: InterVarsity, 2006), 308.

3. John D. Barry and Rebecca Van Noord, *Connect the Testaments: A 365-Day Devotional with Bible Reading Plan* (Bellingham, WA: Lexham Press, 2012).

we give thanks to God, the Father of our Lord Jesus Christ. 4 For we have heard

Christ Jesus and your love for all of God's people, 5 which come from your conf

God has reserved for you in heaven. You have had this expectation ever since yo

he truth of the Good News. 6 This same Good News that came to you is going out a

t is bearing fruit everywhere by changing lives, just as it changed your lives f

t heard and understood the truth about God's wonderful grace. 7 You learned ab

om Epaphras, our beloved co-worker. He is Christ's faithful servant, and he is h

behalf. 8 He has told us about the love for others that the Holy Spirit has give

not stopped praying for you since we first heard about you. We ask God to give y

ge of his will and to give you spiritual wisdom and understanding. 10 Then the

l always honor and please the Lord, and your lives will produce every kind of g

while, you will grow as you learn to know God better and better. 11 We also pray

strengthened with all his glorious power so you will have all the endurance a

d. May you be filled with joy, 12 always thanking the Father. He has enabled you

nheritance that belongs to his people, who live in the light. 13 For he has rescu

gdom of darkness and transferred us into the Kingdom of his dear Son, 14 who pu

and forgave our sins. 15 Christ is the visible image of the invisible God. He ex

g was created and is supreme over all creation, 16 for through him God created

eavenly realms and on earth. He made the things we can see and the things we c

thrones, kingdoms, rulers, and authorities in the unseen world. Everything wa

him and for him. 17 He existed before anything else, and he holds all creation

s also the head of the church, which is his body. He is the beginning, supreme

m the dead. So he is first in everything. 19 For God in all his fullness was ple

t, 20 and through him God reconciled everything to himself. He made peace wit

en and on earth by means of Christ's blood on the cross. 21 This includes you wh

from God. You were his enemies, separated from him by your evil thoughts and

ow he has reconciled you to himself through the death of Christ in his physica

, he has brought you into his own presence, and you are holy and blameless as

im without a single fault. 23 But you must continue to believe this truth and

n't drift away from the assurance you received when you heard the Good News.

s been preached all over the world, and I, Paul, have been appointed as God's s

m it. 24 I am glad when I suffer for you in my body, for I am participating in the

t that continue for his body, the church. 25 God has given me the responsibilit

rch by proclaiming his entire message to you. 26 This message was kept secret

erations past, but now it has been revealed to God's people. 27 For God wanted

About the Author

MIKELLA VAN DYKE is a wife, mother, and the founder of Chasing Sacred, a ministry that provides resources to help women study the Bible and grow closer to God. What began as a devotional blog became an organization with a team of writers who produce theologically rich Bible study resources. She has a master's in practical theology from Regent University, where she fell deeply in love with the process of hermeneutics and wanted to share her knowledge and love of the Word with others. She coleads Bible studies at her local church and enjoys speaking and sharing God's Word at conferences and retreats. She and her husband, Jamie, live in New Hampshire with their five kids, and she's often found riding a four-wheeler or reading the Bible with them.

we give thanks to God, the Father of our Lord Jesus Christ. 4 For we have hear

Christ Jesus and your love for all of God's people, 5 which come from your con

God has reserved for you in heaven. You have had this expectation ever since y

ne truth of the Good News. 6 This same Good News that came to you is going out a

t is bearing fruit everywhere by changing lives, just as it changed your lives :

t heard and understood the truth about God's wonderful grace. 7 You learned a

om Epaphras, our beloved co-worker. He is Christ's faithful servant, and he is

behalf. 8 He has told us about the love for others that the Holy Spirit has give

not stopped praying for you since we first heard about you. We ask God to give

ge of his will and to give you spiritual wisdom and understanding. 10 Then the

l always honor and please the Lord, and your lives will produce every kind of

while, you will grow as you learn to know God better and better. 11 We also pra

strengthened with all his glorious power so you will have all the endurance a

l. May you be filled with joy, 12 always thanking the Father. He has enabled yo

nheritance that belongs to his people, who live in the light. 13 For he has resc

rdom of darkness and transferred us into the Kingdom of his dear Son, 14 who pu

and forgave our sins. 15 Christ is the visible image of the invisible God. He e

g was created and is supreme over all creation, 16 for through him God created

eavenly realms and on earth. He made the things we can see and the things we

thrones, kingdoms, rulers, and authorities in the unseen world. Everything wa

him and for him. 17 He existed before anything else, and he holds all creation

s also the head of the church, which is his body. He is the beginning, supreme

m the dead. So he is first in everything. 19 For God in all his fullness was ple

t, 20 and through him God reconciled everything to himself. He made peace wit

en and on earth by means of Christ's blood on the cross. 21 This includes you wh

from God. You were his enemies, separated from him by your evil thoughts and

ow he has reconciled you to himself through the death of Christ in his physica

, he has brought you into his own presence, and you are holy and blameless as

aim without a single fault. 23 But you must continue to believe this truth and s

on't drift away from the assurance you received when you heard the Good News.

s been preached all over the world, and I, Paul, have been appointed as God's se

n it. 24 I am glad when I suffer for you in my body, for I am participating in the

t that continue for his body, the church. 25 God has given me the responsibility

rch by proclaiming his entire message to you. 26 This message was kept secret

erations past, but now it has been revealed to God's people. 27 For God wanted t

riches and glory of Christ are for you Gentiles, too. And this is the secret:

Join Mikella Van Dyke as she unpacks what it truly means to chase after God.

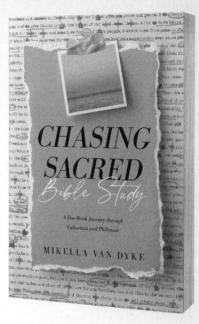

In *Chasing Sacred*, Mikella Van Dyke breaks down the misconceptions and reservations so many of us have about what it means to study the Bible and helps readers learn a practical, step-by-step approach to understanding God's Word.

In the *Chasing Sacred Bible Study*, Mikella will help you unpack God's Word in a new way, using the Inductive Bible Study method to teach a systematic, empowering approach.

Accompanying streaming video available at TyndaleChristianResources.com.

we give thanks to God, the Father of our Lord Jesus Christ. 4 For we have heard

Christ Jesus and your love for all of God's people, 5 which come from your confi

God has reserved for you in heaven. You have had this expectation ever since yo

he truth of the Good News. 6 This same Good News that came to you is going out a

t is bearing fruit everywhere by changing lives, just as it changed your lives f

st heard and understood the truth about God's wonderful grace. 7 You learned ab

om Epaphras, our beloved co-worker. He is Christ's faithful servant, and he is h

behalf. 8 He has told us about the love for others that the Holy Spirit has give

not stopped praying for you since we first heard about you. We ask God to give

ge of his will and to give you spiritual wisdom and understanding. 10 Then the

ll always honor and please the Lord, and your lives will produce every kind of

while, you will grow as you learn to know God better and better. 11 We also pray

strengthened with all his glorious power so you will have all the endurance a

d. May you be filled with joy, 12 always thanking the Father. He has enabled yo

nheritance that belongs to his people, who live in the light. 13 For he has resc

gdom of darkness and transferred us into the Kingdom of his dear Son, 14 who pu

and forgave our sins. 15 Christ is the visible image of the invisible God. He ex

g was created and is supreme over all creation, 16 for through him God created

eavenly realms and on earth. He made the things we can see and the things we c

thrones, kingdoms, rulers, and authorities in the unseen world. Everything wa

him and for him. 17 He existed before anything else, and he holds all creation

s also the head of the church, which is his body. He is the beginning, supreme

m the dead. So he is first in everything. 19 For God in all his fullness was ple

st, 20 and through him God reconciled everything to himself. He made peace wit

en and on earth by means of Christ's blood on the cross. 21 This includes you wh

y from God. You were his enemies, separated from him by your evil thoughts and

ow he has reconciled you to himself through the death of Christ in his physica

t, he has brought you into his own presence, and you are holy and blameless as

him without a single fault. 23 But you must continue to believe this truth and

on't drift away from the assurance you received when you heard the Good News.

s been preached all over the world, and I, Paul, have been appointed as God's s

m it. 24 I am glad when I suffer for you in my body, for I am participating in the

st that continue for his body, the church. 25 God has given me the responsibilit

rch by proclaiming his entire message to you. 26 This message was kept secret

erations past, but now it has been revealed to God's people. 27 For God wanted

CHASING SACRED

Teaching Women How to Study the Bible

Bible Studies
Journals
E-courses
Blog
& More

WE EQUIP WOMEN
WITH SOUND THEOLOGY AND DOCTRINE
TO PROPERLY READ, INTERPRET, AND
APPLY THE TEACHING OF THE BIBLE.

Follow us on Instagram

@chasingsacred

Visit our Website

ChasingSacred.com

CP1978

...d we give thanks to God, the Father of our Lord Jesus Christ. 4 For we have heard

. Christ Jesus and your love for all of God's people, 5 which come from your conf

God has reserved for you in heaven. You have had this expectation ever since yo

he truth of the Good News. 6 This same Good News that came to you is going out a

t is bearing fruit everywhere by changing lives, just as it changed your lives f

t heard and understood the truth about God's wonderful grace. 7 You learned ab

m Epaphras, our beloved co-worker. He is Christ's faithful servant, and he is h

behalf. 8 He has told us about the love for others that the Holy Spirit has give

not stopped praying for you since we first heard about you. We ask God to give y

ge of his will and to give you spiritual wisdom and understanding. 10 Then the

l always honor and please the Lord, and your lives will produce every kind of g

while, you will grow as you learn to know God better and better. 11 We also pray

strengthened with all his glorious power so you will have all the endurance an

d. May you be filled with joy, 12 always thanking the Father. He has enabled you

nheritance that belongs to his people, who live in the light. 13 For he has rescu

gdom of darkness and transferred us into the Kingdom of his dear Son, 14 who pu

and forgave our sins. 15 Christ is the visible image of the invisible God. He ex

g was created and is supreme over all creation, 16 for through him God created

eavenly realms and on earth. He made the things we can see and the things we c

thrones, kingdoms, rulers, and authorities in the unseen world. Everything wa

him and for him. 17 He existed before anything else, and he holds all creation

s also the head of the church, which is his body. He is the beginning, supreme

m the dead. So he is first in everything. 19 For God in all his fullness was ple

t, 20 and through him God reconciled everything to himself. He made peace wit

en and on earth by means of Christ's blood on the cross. 21 This includes you wh

y from God. You were his enemies, separated from him by your evil thoughts and

ow he has reconciled you to himself through the death of Christ in his physica

, he has brought you into his own presence, and you are holy and blameless as y

im without a single fault. 23 But you must continue to believe this truth and

n't drift away from the assurance you received when you heard the Good News.

s been preached all over the world, and I, Paul, have been appointed as God's s

m it. 24 I am glad when I suffer for you in my body, for I am participating in the

t that continue for his body, the church. 25 God has given me the responsibilit

rch by proclaiming his entire message to you. 26 This message was kept secret

erations past, but now it has been revealed to God's people. 27 For God wanted

Life Transformation through Bible Translation

Did you know there are more than 7,000 languages in the world? Unfortunately, about 1,200 of those language communities—representing approximately 100 million people—do not have a single verse of Scripture in words they best understand. Seed Company is a Bible translation organization working to change that.

Believing the Bible is living, active, and relevant for all people, in all cultures, for all time (Hebrews 4:12; 2 Timothy 3:16; 1 Peter 1:23-25), Seed Company partners with other translation organizations and translators—local to their own communities—to see God's Word transforming lives, in every language, in this generation. When people have access to Scripture in the words they think in and dream in, they finally understand that God knows them and loves them.

Just ask Pedro. This 66-year-old speaker of a lesser-known language in South America has attended several Bible translation workshops where Scripture is being translated for his community. Not only has his understanding of God's Word increased, but he longs to teach gospel truth to the next generation. He joyfully reports, "I understand that we do not worship a dead God, but a living and great God." Seed Company is grateful to be working in more than 900 languages to see others like Pedro embracing the hope and truth of Scripture.

Learn more at seedcompany.com

 Seed Company

Photography by Grant Daniels

CP1979

d we give thanks to God, the Father of our Lord Jesus Christ. 4 For we have hear

n Christ Jesus and your love for all of God's people, 5 which come from your conf

God has reserved for you in heaven. You have had this expectation ever since y

he truth of the Good News. 6 This same Good News that came to you is going out a

It is bearing fruit everywhere by changing lives, just as it changed your lives

st heard and understood the truth about God's wonderful grace. 7 You learned a

rom Epaphras, our beloved co-worker. He is Christ's faithful servant, and he is

behalf. 8 He has told us about the love for others that the Holy Spirit has give

e not stopped praying for you since we first heard about you. We ask God to give

dge of his will and to give you spiritual wisdom and understanding. 10 Then the

ll always honor and please the Lord, and your lives will produce every kind of

e while, you will grow as you learn to know God better and better. 11 We also pra

strengthened with all his glorious power so you will have all the endurance a

ed. May you be filled with joy, 12 always thanking the Father. He has enabled yo

inheritance that belongs to his people, who live in the light. 13 For he has resc

gdom of darkness and transferred us into the Kingdom of his dear Son, 14 who p

n and forgave our sins. 15 Christ is the visible image of the invisible God. He e

g was created and is supreme over all creation, 16 for through him God created

heavenly realms and on earth. He made the things we can see and the things we

thrones, kingdoms, rulers, and authorities in the unseen world. Everything w

h him and for him. 17 He existed before anything else, and he holds all creation

is also the head of the church, which is his body. He is the beginning, supreme

om the dead. So he is first in everything. 19 For God in all his fullness was pl

st, 20 and through him God reconciled everything to himself. He made peace wi

ven and on earth by means of Christ's blood on the cross. 21 This includes you wh

y from God. You were his enemies, separated from him by your evil thoughts and

now he has reconciled you to himself through the death of Christ in his physic

t, he has brought you into his own presence, and you are holy and blameless as

him without a single fault. 23 But you must continue to believe this truth and

on't drift away from the assurance you received when you heard the Good News.

as been preached all over the world, and I, Paul, have been appointed as God's s

m it. 24 I am glad when I suffer for you in my body, for I am participating in th

st that continue for his body, the church. 25 God has given me the responsibili

rch by proclaiming his entire message to you. 26 This message was kept secret

erations past, but now it has been revealed to God's people. 27 For God wanted

d we give thanks to God, the Father of our Lord Jesus Christ. 4 For we have hea

Christ Jesus and your love for all of God's people, 5 which come from your co

God has reserved for you in heaven. You have had this expectation ever since

he truth of the Good News. 6 This same Good News that came to you is going out

It is bearing fruit everywhere by changing lives, just as it changed your lives

st heard and understood the truth about God's wonderful grace. 7 You learned

om Epaphras, our beloved co-worker. He is Christ's faithful servant, and he is

behalf. 8 He has told us about the love for others that the Holy Spirit has giv

not stopped praying for you since we first heard about you. We ask God to give

dge of his will and to give you spiritual wisdom and understanding. 10 Then th

ll always honor and please the Lord, and your lives will produce every kind of

while, you will grow as you learn to know God better and better. 11 We also pra

strengthened with all his glorious power so you will have all the endurance a

d. May you be filled with joy, 12 always thanking the Father. He has enabled yo

nheritance that belongs to his people, who live in the light. 13 For he has resc

gdom of darkness and transferred us into the Kingdom of his dear Son, 14 who p

n and forgave our sins. 15 Christ is the visible image of the invisible God. He e

g was created and is supreme over all creation, 16 for through him God created,

heavenly realms and on earth. He made the things we can see and the things we

thrones, kingdoms, rulers, and authorities in the unseen world. Everything w

n him and for him. 17 He existed before anything else, and he holds all creatio

is also the head of the church, which is his body. He is the beginning, supreme

om the dead. So he is first in everything. 19 For God in all his fullness was pl

st, 20 and through him God reconciled everything to himself. He made peace wi

en and on earth by means of Christ's blood on the cross. 21 This includes you wh

y from God. You were his enemies, separated from him by your evil thoughts and

ow he has reconciled you to himself through the death of Christ in his physic

t, he has brought you into his own presence, and you are holy and blameless as

him without a single fault. 23 But you must continue to believe this truth and

on't drift away from the assurance you received when you heard the Good News.

as been preached all over the world, and I, Paul, have been appointed as God's s

m it. 24 I am glad when I suffer for you in my body, for I am participating in th

st that continue for his body, the church. 25 God has given me the responsibilit

rch by proclaiming his entire message to you. 26 This message was kept secret

erations past, but now it has been revealed to God's people. 27 For God wanted

riches and glory of Christ are for you Gentiles, too. And this is the secret: